Contents

THE SKILLS OF MANAGEMENT

A. N. Welsh

Gower

Published by Gower Press, Teakfield Limited,
Reprinted 1982, 1983 by Gower Publishing Company Limited,
Croft Road, Aldershot, Hants, GU11 3HR, England

British Library Cataloguing in Publication Data
Welsh, A. N.
  The skills of management
  1. Management
  I. Title
  658.4   HD31

ISBN 0–566–02171–4

Printed and bound in Great Britain by
Biddles Ltd, Guildford and King's Lynn

Acknowledgements

In the interests of being concise I have made very few references and acknowledgements in this book, and I hope I may be forgiven any omissions. Nevertheless, I must thank Mrs Pat Moss for her many hours of work on the drafts, and Mr David Moss, her husband, of the Plessey Company, who provided much of the inspiration for Chapter 17. I owe a substantial debt to my former employers, W.D. Scott & Company for their forbearance, and for all my experience with them. I must thank Mr Michael Owen and the Air Transport and Travel Industry Training Board for permission to draw from management training material developed while I was with W.D. Scott, and I owe a special debt for encouragement to Philip Stott, Sydney Paulden, Peter Zentner, and to my long-suffering wife Jennifer.

ANW

Introduction

'When all else fails, read the directions.'

Old Chinese Proverb

This book is intended for practising managers and for those who have to understand and assess the management of others. 'Management' in this book means the management of people, how to make them do what you want, how to reconcile the objectives of the enterprise with their own needs and aspirations, and how to use their own time to the best advantage.

The method of the book is to describe practical tips and methods, illustrate them and the learning process, then reinforce by exercises under each subject heading and suggestions for action to be taken. It is appreciated that management is at least partly learned on the job, and that factors such as example, compulsion, and persuasion have to be seen in practice. The book aims at simulating this practice and is, therefore, specific rather than general in most of its areas.

Nevertheless, most good managers know that one of the main secrets of success lies in preparation, and this book may be viewed as a component of the manager's preparation.

The American management writer F. W. Taylor equated management with control and he said that control could only exist in the presence of three prerequisites: firstly, that you should know what your staff *should* be doing, secondly, that they know how they *should* be doing it, and thirdly, that they should know how long it *should* take. This book will be concerned with the will to manage and the will to be managed but it will treat all Taylor's prerequisites in some depth.

Observers of the British management scene will be uncomfortably aware that all too many executives are not able to give a clear answer as to what they should be doing, how and why they should be doing it, and to what sort of timetable. Perhaps one of the biggest problems that results from this is that the individual manager begins to feel that his scope is limited, and as a result he loses confidence. If this book can make it possible for some of that confidence to return by showing managers just how they can achieve difficult or seemingly impossible tasks then its purposes would have been achieved.

The book is in three parts. The first part is the organisation of the manager as a person, how he makes best use of himself and his time, how he improves his decision taking, and how he relates to other people. The second part relates to the actual mechanics of management, how the manager directs his function to achieve results, how he organises tasks, discussion, meetings and reports, and makes or receives communications above and below. The third part is a mixture of techniques which the manager may find helpful in his executive capacity. These include financial and manpower controls and statistics, organisation and method techniques, selling, teaching, and assessment of output.

There are seventeen chapters and it would take you approximately half an hour to read each one and half an hour to complete the exercises at the end; in a complex area the exercises might take one to two hours. Why not work out a reading plan for yourself based on spending one evening, or early morning, or whenever you can *regularly* make the time free, for the next seventeen weeks? Complete one section at a time, do not leave a chapter half finished, but do not burden yourself by trying to do more than one at a time. You can use the chart opposite to keep track of your progress.

This book is a distillation of a great deal of experience and of management development work; if you work through as suggested you will have done as much for yourself at a low cost than you would by attendance at many of the more highly publicised management courses.

One point I should like to add. Increasing numbers of women are obtaining supervisory and managerial positions, and this book is for them also. I may have appeared to address my remarks to men, but this is because of the nature of our English language, where, for better or worse, and as in other circumstances, the masculine embraces the feminine.

STUDY PLAN

Chap-ter	Subject	Time to read (hrs)	Time for exer-cises (hrs)	Date planned	Date actual	Review/re-read

STUDY PLAN (*continued*)

Chap-ter	Subject	Time to read (hrs)	Time for exer-cises (hrs)	Date planned	Date actual	Review/ re-read

Part I

Managing yourself

1 Personal organisation I

'Read not to contradict or confute, nor to believe and take for granted; nor to find talk and discourse; but to weigh and consider'.

Bacon

The need for personal organisation

When I had my first managerial job, I found it naturally very exciting and very demanding. I would come in on or before time, and to digress, a good manager should sometimes come in before time and perhaps stay after time. All sorts of things happen outside normal working hours such as those persons who get their work wrong or do not complete it within the day will stay behind or come back later to finish off, others will use company facilities for private purposes. However, I would come in on or before time and work like mad throughout the day, and by the end I had never completed all that had to be done and my head was full of all that was happening. In particular, I was concerned by matters affecting the well-being of others, and also attacks on my department's activities or my own standards of performance.

When I arrived home my head was buzzing and I would find that I

would wake up in the middle of the night remembering things I had
forgotten to do or thinking of new ideas. I had the choice then of
lying awake during the rest of the night remembering whatever it
was, or going to sleep again and forgetting the matter although I had
not forgotten it. At least I did not decide to hold a meeting about the
situation!

Creating a list

I listed all the jobs which I had to do, all the work in my in-tray and
the functions which I had to supervise. I kept a diary, and a
brought-forward file. The latter in my case was a concertina file with
slots for the days 1 – 31 and for the remaining months of the year. I
would pop into the brought-forward file any correspondence,
assessments, buying orders and the like which I wanted to review at
a future date; these items were brought into the list as they 'came
up'. Having made the first rough list, I then sorted it into order of
importance and urgency. At the end of each day I used to go
through the list and cross off what I had done and also any items
which had ceased to be relevant. I would add to the list any new jobs
or problems which had arisen and then I would note which jobs I
planned to do the following day.

In the morning there was my list telling me what I had to do that
day. Obviously unexpected matters arose – in an operational situation one can almost budget for the unexpected – but by and large I
worked through the list each day.

Communications

One of the standing items on the list, apart from going through the
diary and brought forward file, was to see *all my subordinates*. I kept
at hand a list of all subordinates and made a point of seeing each one
even if only to say 'hello', every day. It could be, of course, that you
are often away, or that you have too many staff to see. Perhaps in
the first case you should consider whether you are away too much to
do your job properly; in the second case either you may have too
many people directly under you or should delegate some of the
communication process to subordinates. Communications is the

name of this game: people require *regular contact* and in particular from their boss, and they will often say things, or you will be able to sense a problem which they would be diffident to bring to your office.

As an aside, what does your office look like to a subordinate? Can he come and obtain access to you, or are you involved most of the time in meetings, deep discussions or telephone calls? Communications can only exist on face-to-face basis, and they are of prime importance at every level. Many managers with considerable responsibilities in large organisations do not know the names or faces of their top management and directors. An even greater proportion never see, or are seen by, their top management in any operational situation from year to year end. *No amount of personnel work can make people think you care about them if they never see you.*

Personal planning

The first list of work is much more difficult to produce than the subsequent amendments, and to help you produce it there is a list of questions on p.6. These are general and analytical questions to be used in any review of your responsibilities, but they would assist in preparing the first list. When, you may ask, would you ever have time to do this, and is it possible with everyone rampaging around and the phone ringing?

However, do you intend to spend the rest of your life in a managerial pigsty, and are you seriously going to say you are too busy to do your job? Half an hour of planning or forethought saves hours or days of misdirected effort; the crisis anticipated is no panic, and you should find in the normal situation that if you pursue this type of personal planning for a few months, you will get right 'ahead of the game', and that you can start looking for additional responsibilities.

Decide now on a specific half hour in the coming week to go through the list. Ask someone else to take the calls and say you do not want to be disturbed (unless it is the Chairman!). Some of the questions will be the subject of later chapters in the book or require further investigation, but whenever the answer you reach is other than satisfactory, then answer the following question: '*What am I going to do about it?'*

One common situation is that old sinking feeling that while problems could be put right if only one had the time – one never has and never will have. The subsequent chapter offers some suggestions on this point.

Checklist for reviewing your function

1 What are the objectives of my department or function?
2 Am I satisfied that I feel these can be achieved – that I have a plan/s for this?
3 In what ways can my department or area be improved?
4 Is the work in my area altering in nature, quantity, or quality?
5 Can the work be done in a better way?
6 Have I the right equipment and facilities?
7 Have I the right number of staff?
8 Am I happy that all my subordinates are correctly placed and loaded?
9 Are my staff doing what I want them to do?
10 Do any of my staff need further training or experience? Have I a training plan?
11 What are staffing trends?
12 Are my staff happy? Do I spend enough time with them?
13 Have I trained a deputy?
14 Am I satisfied personally? Have I defined my personal objectives?
15 Is my authority defined and adequate?
16 Is my relationship with my senior management satisfactory?
17 Where is my next promotion coming from?
18 Am I doing too much routine or adminstrative clerical work?
19 Have I enough time for thinking?

2 Personal organisation II

'The slothful man saith, there is a lion without, I shall be slain in the street.'

Proverbs XXV

The constraint of time

The best manager is the one who manages best. Managing is not easy, and it is conducted within a large number of constraints. What is your biggest constraint? Is it capital, working finance, material resources, machinery, property or is it people? People can be a big limiting factor, but you can always train them. Are you limited by the presence of other aspects? Many factors can constrain you, but *the biggest restriction of all is your own time*. You never have enough of it. There are only 24 hours in a day, 7 days in a week, 52 weeks in the year and so many years in your career. You cannot produce more time; it keeps slipping away. Yesterday can never come back.

We would say, therefore, that we do not have as much time as we need, but would this be equally true for everybody, or would it apply in particular to you? Time can be replaced. Certain tasks can be performed by machinery and certain office work can be done by computers. Some tasks can be delegated to other people, although this is really a transfer of time. However, *the manager cannot delegate his management work* to a machine and seldom can he share it with anyone else. There is no substitute for time as far as he is concerned. Everything he does takes time. All business, all activity, all work uses time and takes place in time.

However, we do not manage our time naturally – as a whole we take it for granted. Now we could talk for a long time about this problem, and we could say that the unhurried, unheroic manager with a clear desk, and a reliable organised office is the efficient or effective manager, but what do you do about it?

Step 1

Accept that other things being equal, *the best and happiest manager* is the one who *makes the best use of his time*. If you do not accept this, then this chapter was not written for you, but if you feel that you can make better use of time, and that if you do so you will be a better manager, then please read on.

Step 2

This comprises finding out what you are doing now. A simple method of doing this is to list various activities which you perform, and record for a week or a fortnight how long you are spending on them. This can be done by using a simple daily diary sheet; the diary sheets are analysed into what is called a work distribution chart at the end of the period. The work distribution chart will show quite clearly what you are doing and what proportion of your time you are spending on your various activities (see Figure 14.1).

A specimen managers' activity list, with the activities given for example only, is as follows:

1 Visiting customers.
2 Visiting suppliers.
3 Queries from staff over technical matters.
4 Customer complaints.
5 Planning and control work.
6 Training.
7 Supervision.
8 Reading mail.
9 Chasing overdue accounts.

10 Checking stocks and reordering.
11 Management meetings.
12 Recruiting.
13 Staff problems.
14 Personal.

Simple forms for the diary sheet and work distribution chart are shown in Figs. 2.1 and 2.2.

The work of a manager is variable, particularly as regards the subject involved. A work distribution chart exercise will not give a 100 per cent accurate picture of what the manager does or should do, but it will give a representative view of the proportions of his

Date:

Time	Activity	Inter-ruptions	Phone calls	1. Inessen-tial	2. Some-body else could do	3. Wast-ing others time	Notes
8.30 8.45 9.00 9.15 9.30 9.45 10.00 ,, ,, ,, ,, 5.30 5.45 6.00 Evening	Enter number against time whenever activity changes.	Enter a '1' for each, e.g. 1, 11	As for interruptions. Note incidence and quantity. Analyse if too many.	Record impressions, if any, at the time.	Record impressions, if any, at the time.	Record impressions, if any, at the time.	Note anything unusual or 'special'.

Fig. 2.1 Specimen managers' diary sheet

Activity no.	Activity title	Daily times										Total time	% of total	Comments and action
		1	2	3	4	5	1	2	3	4	5			
														(You can also do this kind of analysis with your staff.)
														These are taken to the nearest quarter hour.
	Interruptions. Phone calls.										(No)	(No)		If phone calls and interruptions occur which are separate from the activity being recorded – multiply by 3 minutes; if the total exceed 15% of the day, then analyse them. Possibly something is wrong.

time spent on various activities, e.g. queries; accounts queries may relate to different transactions, but they will still be accounts queries. Once the work distribution chart has been completed, one can then move on to the next step.

Step 3

The third step is the analysis of the work distribution chart. A number of questions need to be asked at this stage.

Wasted time

1 What would happen if I did not do this kind of activity?
2 Am I spending too long on it?
3 Am I doing it ineffectively – for example, am I getting it properly set up and spending enough time on it? Short periods of supervision are of limited value with persons engaged on complex work.
4 Am I failing to do any task which would contribute to the business because of lack of time?

Supervision

A manager should be able to spend time with his staff – encouraging, training, supervising and just getting to know them and keeping in touch. The time required for this varies with the staff and the complexity of the work, but a rough quick figure is an average of forty minutes per person per day. This includes normal management duties, reports and 'personnel' work. It does not include 'checking' as distinct from normal supervision and training.

Checking

Checking should be considered carefully. Twenty or thirty years ago commercial convention looked for a high degree of literal accuracy and salary costs were lower in proportion to other expenses than they are now. There is a satisfaction in getting everything 'right' and producing little masterpieces, but we should consider what the customer really wants and needs first. Checking is expensive and frustrating: it is no longer a motivating factor (if it ever was) for staff to have all their work checked.

Your work distribution chart will show how much of your time is spent checking, but you should consider whether the cost of checking is justified by the errors discovered and how much these matter. If the errors do matter you may have to continue the check, but you can consider whether random checks, occasional, unexpected checks, will serve as well where general quality standards and methods are the main concern.

List of jobs

In the end you will finish with a list of the jobs which you want to do and which you have to do, and a subsidiary list of jobs which you feel you should not be doing but perhaps you still have to do for one reason or another. (We are, of course, well aware that you cannot get rid of all inessential tasks, but you can reduce them.) You will *rank the list of jobs in order of importance* to the business, and estimate what general proportion of your time and energy should be spent on each.

You will have considered where time is being wasted on unnecessary work, and where time could be saved by better personal organisation and work methods. You should move to the next heading in your analysis of the work distribution chart.

Delegation

Ask yourself which of your activities could be done by somebody else to an adequate standard, or as well as you, or even better. The manager is paid to do his work, but if there are others at lower salaries who can do part of it and have the time, then is it better for the manager to be fully occupied or for the junior staff?

Another factor which comes out of this analysis is that the more senior people become, the larger becomes the proportion of their time spent on moving about and travelling, and you should think about this.

There will be certain customers who are very important, and who are accustomed to dealing with you personally; it may well be that you can introduce them to someone else who can deal with the routine parts of the account but, of course, you will remember to watch what is happening to the account from time to time subsequent to this arrangement. This would apply also to 'important jobs' and to important senior managers!

A few years back the managing directors of several major companies in the United Kingdom were in very humble positions; in fact, consider where you yourself were five years ago, and now you are performing much more important work. Quite possibly within your area you have the managers or senior managers of the future, and you should keep a look out for them and give them a 'chance' as soon as you can. Not only will this be good for them, but it will also free you. Think about how to develop the business and to perform your other managerial tasks.

One thing which is very irksome to staff is to see people senior to them performing activities at greater salaries which they could perfectly well do themselves. In one major British company staff are asked the question 'What does your supervisor do that you could do yourself?' Could you ask this question of your staff, and would they know how to answer it? It is worth considering that they may have views on this subject themselves.

Subordinates' time

A manager becomes a manager by promotion or appointment. He learns to be a manager by observing other managers, who themselves have been taught by observation, and show how, and from what is called the 'hard way'. There are certain training courses, but they are normally very short, and as a result most managers devise their style and system of management from their own experience. Often this is very good, but once personal inclinations creep in, funny things start to happen.

You should ask yourself the following question: 'Is there anything I do which wastes subordinates' time without contributing to their effectiveness?' You can begin to answer this question from your analysis of the work distribution chart, and you may even be able to ask it of the subordinates themselves.

Waiting around

The type of event we have in mind is where your staff have to hang around waiting for answers from you, items to be checked or approved, action to be taken, or for you to be available? Consider whether in your area you ever have two or more people involved in work which should be done by one person only. Normally speaking, it is more satisfying and efficient for a job which can be done by one person to be done by one person and not split between two or three. Staff learn from observing you (or colleagues), but sometimes you may be playing to an audience unnecessarily (and distracting the others).

Remember when you were a member of the staff or a worker. Did your manager or foreman ever waste any of your time while you waited around for him to be available, when he was late, when he had to check your work, while he had to get around to this or that but was (or allowed himself to be) interrupted by a variety of other matters? Did this frustrate you as well as waste your time? Staff are paid less than managers, but with overheads, the difference is not as great as it once was. Are you working too hard; are you paying the proverbial dog then doing the barking yourself?

Crises

One thing which wastes time, particularly of subordinates, is where there is a crisis. In many organisations crises occur regularly, and there are so many things which are unforeseen that one could almost describe crises as a routine situation. However, a recurrent crisis is a symptom of slovenliness and laziness. Certain crises such as making up the returns, the budget figures, sales figures, payroll, the peak season are all known in advance. If the manager uses some of the techniques suggested in Chapter 6, he may well be able to provide for these, in which case they will become routine occurrences and not crises.

Panic action is expensive. People rushing off to make special deliveries, special visits to the post office, special trips out to acquire stationery, other things that are needed, people dropping things in the middle of picking up others and so on, all lead to ineffective use of time and also mistakes.

Improvements

The question here is, how can you use your time more effectively?

The first thing to consider is what is your attention span. Are you a person who works best by sitting down quietly and for extended periods looking at a particular problem, or do you keep things running around in your mind? What are your best methods of working, and with whom and when?

Discretionary time

You need to have a certain amount of 'discretionary time', i.e. time at your free disposal, time available for important matters, perhaps the things you are paid for, and this must be kept in usable chunks. Not many managers feel they have much discretionary time, even after cutting out any wasted time, but they can generally set aside an hour or so each week. The question arises as to how much discretionary time is desirable. This is rather like the maintenance situation on a car; you do not buy a car in order to service it, but if you do not carry out a certain amount of maintenance on the car it will not perform satisfactorily.

Your function

The same applies to your function. You need from time to time to review the total operation of your area and to go through the check list given previously on page 6; you need to make sure you see the staff regularly and review their situation. On a daily basis you may want to keep a list of the tasks which you have to do, and the problems with deadlines and priorities, and perhaps revise these either last thing at night or first thing in the morning. Also you may well want to use a brought-forward file or diary system so that you are automatically reminded of things that need doing in the future. How long this should take is like the service on the car, except that it is you rather than the garage that must make the diagnosis and the decisions.

Suggestions

Simple suggestions for using your time more effectively are to concentrate on one thing at a time; deal with first things first, and one at a time. Allow enough time for what you are doing – nothing ever goes completely right and one thing you can always expect is the unexpected. Do not hurry, do not try and do several things at once. Do not assume that everything that was important yesterday is important today. Ask yourself the question 'If we had not already started on this activity would we start it now?' It is just as difficult and just as risky to do something small as something which is big, so allocate your time to the most important parts of the business.

When you have analysed your work distribution chart comparing the proportions of time spent on the various activities with their importance in terms of obtaining income, business and profit or other advantage for the company, you will most certainly find that you are spending a lot of your time on small irritating matters. Consider whether some of these can be allowed to slide without damage to the business, and whether things would be improved by concentrating on the managerial areas of the business.

Summary

To sum up, this chapter has offered certain suggestions for work on your own position. It has been suggested that the better manager is the better organised manager, who makes best use of his time and best use of the time of his staff. However, just as there is no such thing as a born manager, so the effectiveness of a good manager cannot really be taught. *Effectiveness has to be learned* and the suggestions in this chapter are only some pointers as to how one can look at one's work, develop a style and personal approach and make the best use of one's time.

3 Management and leadership styles

Definition of a manager: 'one who pats you on the back in front of your face, and then hits you below the belt behind your back'.

Looking back

My industrial career started in the early 1950s and as I remember life then, and it is not so long ago, a discussion on management styles would have been an unusual matter. Work was under way on the behavioural aspects of business organisation, e.g. Blake, Douglas McGregor, Maslow, Herzberg, etc., but from a day-to-day point of view, management seemed a more obvious thing than it does now.

Business has grown more complex and complicated, but I started with some of Britain's larger organisations. At that time a manager, whether he was an office manager, a foreman, a works manager, an executive director, etc., was a more recognisable entity. At different levels managers had little ways of dressing and behaving appropriate to their rank and status. The use of 'sirs', 'misters', initials and ways of speaking and being spoken to were much more formalised than they are today. In private life one's style tended to reflect one's grade, and wives were just as conscious of the pecking order as anyone else.

There were less qualifications around, but again they seemed to command more attention, as did the possession of private wealth, connections (and titles) and an expensive education. In insurance the top jobs were reserved for actuaries; in chemical manufacture, chemists; in engineering, engineers, etc., though even in those days a good arts graduate or a clever accountant might overtake on the outside lane.

Everyone, from the lowest to the highest, behaved with deference and in many cases real respect to those above them, and instructions were treated with a degree of loyalty and alacrity which may have been a hangover from the wartime (and from difficult times before the war).

I am not looking back with a rosy view of those days. We moved, as I remember it, with much less precision than we do now. Many managers would be considered irresponsibly lazy or incompetent by today's standards in almost every way, but they were managers.

Today's managers

And now, today, who are the managers? There is much to suggest that the manager is beginning to lose his or her identity. Real power is moving away from the middle and junior echelons as top management (much improved in quality), much better supplied with information and evaluations through the use of advanced techniques and electronic data processing systems, tends to make the real decisions. At the other end the unions represent the power of organised labour, but even where no union exists, the employee, backed by recent legislation and the shortage of skilled labour, is, even in times of high unemployment, in a far stronger position than ever before.

Managers, seeing a top management/union power axis on the one hand, and a confusing array of specialist and professional staff also of managerial status on the other, are moving from a 'manager' position old-style to a sort of executive grey area. Frustration and powerlessness set in and the manager seeks to reidentify himself, turning frequently to the pursuit of a management charisma, a Pied Piper ability, to make things go his way again, a management style for results.

This book offers some suggestions as to what action can be taken in different situations to maximise impact, but it may be worth considering the 'results bit' – what we are managing for? Possibly the key result is our own personal job satisfaction, but we get it through achieving results, and having those results recognised as success.

Various approaches

The framework in which managers are accustomed to operate is similar to that originally developed by the Romans. This is the classical (or 'line and staff') approach, in which a managerial hierarchy was laid down, with clear and symmetrical relationships and job descriptions and authorities at each level. This approach in its more extreme forms is very clear and easily understood – it also facilitates movements from one position to another.

Most firms today operate a 'development' of this but temper it with bits of the other two main approaches to organisation – these are the Human Relations approach, and the Systems approach. The Human Relations approach concerns itself with creating an environment which naturally stimulates or encourages people to work together. Group Technology or the ICI Weekly Staff Agreement, project teams, participative systems, etc., are examples of this. The Systems approach on the other hand, posits that the operation of a business stems from evaluation of information and considers reporting, feedback mechanisms, and communications as of very high importance. Naturally a highly developed data processing system is an essential tool in preparing the business model. Both the human relations and systems approaches are valid and necessary components of organisational design, but they militate against traditional management concepts.

Personal career planning

So, as we put it, how does the manager behave, how is he identified? Is there a managerial or leadership style best suited to produce results?

Historically it would seem that the great pressure to obtain management positions will reduce as these appointments become fewer in number, less well paid in relation to other jobs, and more demanding/less satisfying. Those who stay will need to have defined and developed skills and it will cease to be that the educated or ambitious will naturally move in a great mass through the various management 'levels'.

Initial rules

So what do we need to do? Two initial rules may be suggested. First, to consider Einstein's statement that in an age of large scale events and organisations, the greatest single issue of importance, apart from the question of peace or war, is for the individual to feel that he counts. You *do* matter – to your family and friends, to your company, to yourself, and to God. You are of significance, you can have some influence on events.

The other rule, in the words of the song is: 'If you don't have a dream, then your dream can't come true'. You can go through life reacting to circumstances, taking it as it comes, but there is a danger that you may not find yourself where you had wished to be. How sad if you approach the end of your career realising that you have abilities which have never been fully used, experiences which you have missed, and that opportunities which you would have valued but which have passed you by. Some suggestions for starting to condition and plan your career are given below.

Suggestions for planning your career

Alas, we only live once. Part of your life you have already had, and that leaves a balance between time now, and your expected retirement date. Those precious years are all you have in order to achieve career and business objectives, and as you will spend the preponderance of your waking time in your employment, the progress of your career will be a major influence in your domestic affairs and lifestyle. Therefore, draw a timescale for yourself as shown in Fig. 3.1.

(Birth)   (Time now)   (Retirement) (Death)

```
 |----+----+----+----+----+----+----+----|
 0    10   20   30   40   50   60   70   80
Age
```

Fig. 3.1 Timescale

Next, visualise your retirement party or presentation. Someone who knows you makes a little speech. What is he likely to say about you? What would you want him to be saying out of the following:

(a) the position you have reached;
(b) the kind of person you are;
(c) your relations with your colleagues;
(d) the work you have done;
(e) your special interests.

Perhaps you cannot see so far ahead, but look five, ten years forward. Decide where you want to be, what you want to be earning. If you find your personal objectives unclear, try some analysis of yourself. You do not know what will happen in the future, but you know what has happened in the past. Draw an extra dimension to your timescale as shown in Fig. 3.2.

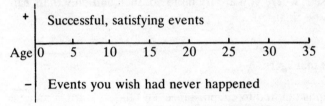

Fig. 3.2 Extra dimension to timescale

Plot in the events which have had the main emotional impact on you. These may be major happenings, winning a prize, good exam results, getting married, your first job, managerial promotion, being sacked, becoming bankrupt, a serious accident, etc., or minor happenings, an argument you regretted, losing a toy, a success in the garden, a day out with the kids. Plot them in, and then perhaps rewrite the figure so that you get a clear picture. If the graph is too crowded, make two lists – the bad and the good.

Analyse the picture and see what characteristics each list, each side of your graph exhibits. What does this tell you about yourself, and how can you aim the rest of your life to have more of the satisfying experiences and less of the undesirable experiences?

Having an objective, or better still, a hierarchy or list of objectives, then you can plan how best to achieve them and over what period.

1 Let others know your aims, wherever possible and wherever tactful! This would include your wife/husband, who will be a

major influence in providing moral support.

2 Find out what qualifications, experience and knowledge will be helpful and make a plan to acquire them.

3 Consider what friends and contacts will be appropriate.

4 Work out the steps required to put you in the most likely position to achieve your objectives and then diarise formal reviews of the .situation. Sit down every three months, for example, and compare where you are with where you planned, how it looks – are the objectives to be revised (upwards, downwards or sideways) – and what have you done compared with what you planned to do.

You could be asking how personal career planning relates to the subject of this chapter, management and leadership styles. The answer is this, until you have worked out what you are trying to do with yourself, where you are trying to go, then and only then, can your style be finalised.

Successful managers

Leadership is tailored to circumstance, and the style for running a filing system might be inappropriate on the battlefield, or say, in a hotel business. The sales manager, the accountant, and the factory manager all act according to their situations, but they also act according to their personalities. Maybe the two fit, but many successful managers (or managers in successful situations) attribute their success to their personal style. Maybe there is a real correlation, but we all know managers who are successful in spite of their personal styles!

Why are managers successful (luck and ability excepted)? It is because they know what they are doing and why. They know their departmental objectives, the procedures, the facts of the business and they understand and are close to the people around them. They have kept their thought processes working so that they can keep on top of their jobs, ahead of the game. Crises and panics have been anticipated so that when the level of orders suddenly doubles, or the computer breaks down in the middle of the payroll, there is a plan for taking the necessary action. The department is tidy and well-ordered and there are no nasties under the carpet, no skeletons lurking in the cupboards. A manager who has achieved this will be confident, unstressed, objective and approachable, but perhaps only after he has achieved a measure of the halcyon situation.

The best manager is the manager who manages best, and in general that means achieving the objectives of his function as economically as possible. We have seen and will see that management is a matter of competence and control, and consists largely in taking the right actions rather than in presenting certain styles.

Managers are human beings, and work through and with other human beings. If managers in your company are expected to wear flowered ties, for example, by all means fit the company managerial image, but be yourself. The only way to present a consistent and understandable style over the years is to be true to your own personality – commit your talents to the organisation to whatever extent is necessary, but keep your ego and emotions to yourself.

Summary

To sum up, management is about achieving results and not about particular styles. Leadership is assisted by personal qualities, but its main and indispensable component is competence.

Exercises

1 Draw your own lifespan timescale plan (as in Fig. 3.1) and analyse it as suggested.
2 Determine your career objectives.
3 Write an up-to-date personal history or curriculum vitae as if you were applying for the job you want eventually. List your deficiences and strengths in relation to your objectives.
4 Describe your own management style (as you see it).
5 List three main strengths in your style. Can these be developed and can more use be made of them in the work in which you are involved?
6 List three main weaknesses. Do these affect the results you obtain – and if so, is there anything you can do to overcome your problems or to prevent them affecting your performance?
7 Analyse the styles of the manager you most admire and that of the manager you least admire. Does that tell you anything about

4 Personal impact

Franco was in a coma for several weeks before he died. One afternoon the coma lifted and he heard a murmuring of many voices in the courtyard outside. 'What are those people doing?' he asked his wife, who was at the bedside. 'They are waiting to say Goodbye' she answered. 'Why?' he replied, positive to the last, 'Where are they going?'.

The manager spends his day in the company of other people; they are looking at him, hearing him and relating to him, and, therefore, his personal presentation is very important.

It is easier to work with someone who is pleasant and receptive and who seems businesslike and efficient. This chapter offers some suggestions for keeping your own presentation at its best. I make no apology if some of the points seem like an insult: one has only to look around to be aware of how much room for improvement there is.

Appearance

Are your clothes clean and well cared for? Are they appropriate to the company's style, and to the image you want to present? Are your shoes clean and in good condition?

Is your hair tidy? Is the style suitable for your age and position, and does it help you to appear to your best advantage? Do you pay attention to personal hygiene?

Bearing

If you slouch around, recline in your seat, or put your feet up, etc., you can damage an otherwise good impression. Without appearing too 'military', move briskly and appear to mean business.

Office

Keep your office tidy. Set it up to look efficient and pleasant, to put visitors at their ease and to make transacting business with you a comfortable proceeding. Otherwise dismal surroundings can be transformed by a good clean and some decorations, e.g. window drapes, a picture or a plant. A cluttered desk distracts visitors and is inefficient in itself.

Words

Words are our main medium of communication and they can do a great deal of damage. What is said once can never be unsaid. One of the rules of discussion is never to try to match other people's views, stories, experiences, etc., unless you really can. It is better to be relatively quiet, go away and research and then come back when you have something worthwhile to say. As a manager you will then get the reputation of always having something worthwhile to say.

As a manager you will secure co-operation and understanding best if people like you. If they do not like you, or there is a tendency not to like you, there will be a tension which will cause a filtering of anything which you say to them and, in many cases rejection. It follows that you must have a pleasant speaking manner and say things in a likeable way. Some advice is given in this chapter, but it seems to me that some sessions in front of the company's closed circuit TV apparatus – the present-day equivalent of practising in front of a mirror (or your spouse) – would be helpful.

Ways of speaking

The speaker needs to control any internal tensions involved in the meeting. He must relax, and the way to do this is by deep controlled rhythmic breathing. Passive relaxation is where one lies down with the legs apart (about 30 cm), the feet turned outwards, the hands lying by one's side; the face in particular should be deliberately relaxed. A few minutes in this posture, breathing in for five seconds and out for ten, fifteen or more seconds will set you up for anything.

Active relaxation is when you are actually doing your talking, etc., and you relax all parts of the body other than those which are necessary for the action concerned.

Breathing is very important, and if one breathes correctly one can carry on to the end of a sentence, however long it is; one never becomes hoarse, and one can go on talking even in a situation where considerable projection is necessary, for hours on end, so help us! One expands the rib-cage with the abdomen in, the chest out, the shoulders down. One keeps the rib-cage expanded, and the lungs are contracted by movement by the diaphragm, i.e. solar plexus, so that you breath from the stomach.

It is necessary to get the right balance of carbon dioxide and oxygen. Shallow rapid breathing as employed by athletes (excepting swimmers) increases the intake of carbon dioxide; very slow deep breathing increases the proportion of oxygen and freshens the system, i.e. this enables you to keep a clear head.

Refer back to the suggestion that you practise this type of diaphragmatic breathing, breathing in for five seconds and out more slowly, say ten seconds, then fifteen seconds, etc. The actor's test is to breathe out in front of a lighted candle and not cause the flame to flicker.

One must talk from the front of the face, i.e. immediately behind the top teeth and keep the tongue down. Say 'Ah!' in front of a mirror and see if your tongue follows the line of the bottom of your mouth; if you find it is stuck somewhere up above the middle, it is going to get in the way. Economise on your breathing, no big exhalations or sighs of relief.

Learn to concentrate. Whenever you have a spare moment, concentrate on an object, e.g. an ashtray or a light-fitting, and describe it in such a way that someone else would know what it is, i.e. colour, form, characteristics, associations, materials, components, etc.; think before you speak.

Use of words

It is said there is a correlation between vocabulary, IQ, and success. There are 80,000 words in the *Oxford English Dictionary*, but the average individual uses only 3,500, although he may recognise a larger number. Some groping for the appropriate phrase or word may not matter at certain levels and on certain occasions, but in serious discussions, negotiations and communications it becomes important to be able to express oneself clearly, and with ease. Phrases like 'the chairman was on about expenses again', 'Mr. Smith said something about us looking at the delivery position', 'etcetera, etcetera', 'you know what I mean?' tend to come out involuntarily if one is accustomed to using them.

A suggestion is to pick out five or six words you recognise but do not use, e.g. from a newspaper or book, and endeavour to use them frequently the following week. Practise a further set the subsequent week, and so on, and this will gradually increase your word-power. It is also suggested that anyone who wants to turn ordinary speaking into the true art of suggestion should equip himself with *Roget's Thesaurus, Complete Plain Words* by Sir Ernest Gowers (HMSO or Penguin) and H. W. Fowler's *Dictionary of Modern English Usage* (edited by Sir Ernest Gowers – Oxford University Press), and a good old-fashioned dictionary.

As stated then, speak with a hard palate and a hard stomach. You cannot breathe through your nose when you are talking. This means that if the atmosphere is smoky or otherwise polluted you deny yourself the filtering activities of the nose. If you have to do a lot of talking, do not spend the previous evening talking in a polluted atmosphere. Furthermore, when you are talking, relax and open the back of your throat and this will save undue wear-and-tear on your vocal chords.

Voice interest

The aspect of making your voice interesting and attractive comes under the following headings: phrasing, pauses, pitch, pace, inflection, stress, emphasis and volume. These should all be varied to give interest, but what is needed here is to use the rules mentioned so far (and, of course, substantial preparation), so that one's mind is clear to concentrate on the effect of what one is saying and to how it is being received by the listener. Set or semi-set talks need a great deal of preparation and rehearsal, although when given as, say, an after-dinner speech or a lecture, they may appear completely spontaneous. It is suggested that the same approach is applied to meetings, where one may have to make proposals or responses which can be known or guessed at beforehand. Where matters arise for which you are not prepared, it may be better to avoid trying to answer completely on that occasion.

A word is necessary about dialects. Dialects and particular speech characteristics may be musical and attractive, but the average effect is to make it more difficult for other people to understand you if the accent is different from their own. Furthermore, you may not pronounce certain sounds too clearly. Practise these sounds, your enunciation, tongue twisters, for a few minutes as you drive to work (assuming you have no passengers!).

Effective listening

It is just as important to listen effectively as it is to speak effectively. A few ground rules are offered:

1 Concentrate fully at all times; make a real habit of paying careful attention even if it appears that the speaker is saying something you have heard before or is talking rubbish.
2 Interrupt as little as possible; let people finish what they are going to say – their view on when to stop may be different from yours, and you may cause considerable frustration and misunderstanding if you do not allow them to finish.
3 Offer an open mind and deliberately obliterate your prejudices – this is particularly important when talking to people very much younger or older than yourself, where the effect of being

brought up in a different period leads to different attitudes.

4 Use empathy; put yourself in the other person's shoes and try to analyse what they are driving at, what they are feeling, what they want to communicate – respond by nods, smiles, facial gestures, saying 'yes!', etc., so that they are encouraged to think you are receiving their message.

5 Care for, and appear to care for, and acknowledge other points of view than your own. As you know from experience, life is very seldom black-and-white, and it is quite possible to draw different conclusions, all with some validity, from the same facts and analyses.

6 We should always attempt to respond intelligently and to help the speaker get his points over clearly, even if we are going to subsequently differ from him. We are all tempted to 'put the boot in' from time to time, destroying arguments by wit and sarcasm and other less elegant devices, but this should really be avoided.

5   Objectives

'A well managed plant is a quiet place, a factory that is "dramatic", a factory in which the epic of industry is unfolded before the visitors eyes, is poorly managed. A well managed factory is boring. Nothing exciting happens in it because the crises have been anticipated and been converted into routine.'

P. F. Drucker

Very early in this book we mentioned F.W. Taylor's three prerequisites of control: *the necessity to know what one should be doing, how one should be doing it, and how long it should take.* Much sorrow and uncertainty is caused to the manager by not knowing exactly what he has to be doing, or if he does know what he is doing, he perhaps does not know how much of it he should do, and in what time. The manager should have personal objectives and he should also have company or departmental objectives. One could go further and say that it is very difficult to have a full sense of achievement if one does not know what one is attempting to achieve. It is also difficult to bring oneself to attempt to achieve things which one believes to be impossible. The old adage 'the impossible we do at once, miracles take a little longer' is excellent as a statement of intent but as a task for everyday living it has some shortcomings.

Management by objectives

The technique of management by objectives is one in which the organisation states its clear overall targets and then works out plans, both functionally and for each individual, whereby those plans can be achieved and whereby the achievement of them is monitored by routine reviews. It suits the style of some chief executives and the organisations to which they belong to operate in this controlled and ordered fashion, but it requires a great deal of effort to proceed in this way. The majority of readers of this book will not be in organisations where forward moves are planned or proceed to plan but are in a rather more flexible or dynamic situation. This is not to say that flexibility or dynamism are impossible under MBO, very much the reverse; what we are really saying is that most readers will be from companies where MBO is not in operation.

One of the fundamental needs of people is *the security of knowing where they stand* and what they are trying to do. This is particularly true of the manager who is responsible for human and material resources other than himself. It is axiomatic that to retain his sanity and to make best use of the resources he has available he must be quite clear as to what he is trying to do, how to do it and as said before, how long he has.

Definition of objective

Let us define what we mean by an objective. An objective must be specific, it must be achievable and it must be desirable. Let us quote an example. You are house services manager and part of your operation includes the postroom. The function of the postroom is to deliver the mail; the aim of the postroom is to deliver the mail as quickly as possible; the objective of the postroom might be to deliver the mail by 9 o'clock each morning. That is a very simple statement of an objective and it may be, of course, argued that it is impossible to deliver the mail by 9 o'clock in the morning without increasing the staff of the postroom to an uneconomic extent. It is quite permissible to modify the objective and say to deliver the incoming mail by 9 o'clock in the morning nine days out of ten and by 9.30 a.m. on all occasions. Let us look at that. The objective is specific there, the question of whether it is achievable or not has to be considered, and the question of desirability is also to be considered. It may be that 9 o'clock is the time by which the mail is required and, therefore, to deliver the mail prior to 9 o'clock would not be appropriate. It may be that to close the postroom down entirely and use the premises as, for example a bingo hall, might be very much more profitable but again that might not be desirable.

Standards or targets

Under the heading of objectives we are really talking of a number of standards or targets. It is sometimes said that an individual middle manager cannot really make objectives which affect the company; the company policy whether on a fully planned or partly planned basis is made by others and the manager has to react to the situation as it arises. Of course he has, but the more he is able to control his own department or his own function, the better he will be able to react to changes and also to contribute to the company for which he is working. Most managers have this basic need or compulsion to accept responsibility which is why they are managers. They also need to understand fully their own areas of responsibility where these can contribute and how well they are performing, and to do this they have to learn to think in quantified terms. The managing director has to think in quantified terms, translate these figures on to paper and plan to achieve these results.

Overall objectives

Profits do not happen; they result only if objectives are being achieved in a range of areas, and these are likely to be achieved only if the managing director has done his part. The chief executive, the managing director and the chairman, the board have to consider important matters such as what the company is really in business for and what its objectives are in the short, medium and long term. Whether or not they have done this, the individual manager still has to find targets or standards of operation for his own function. In many cases the manager, whether he be at departmental, branch, divisional or section level, is closest in touch with the customer and with the actual work going on; he is, as it were, at the 'sharp end'. The manager is often better qualified than senior management to know what the customer is likely to accept, what the staff are likely to do and what is viable in particular circumstances. He may well be the best person to recommend objectives or to propose what is feasible in his own area to fit in with an overall company plan, or, as it is suggested in this chapter, to run his own operation or function to the best satisfaction of himself and of the company.

Individual manager

We mentioned some overall organisational objectives but for the individual manager his targets or standards are going to fall under two headings. First of all these will relate to the business and will be operational standards; the second group relate to the staff and resources which are under his control. The functional or operational standards fall under the following headings:

   (a) cost;
   (b) income or turnover;
   (c) quantity;
   (d) speed;
   (e) quality;
   (f) errors;
   (g) service;
   (h) company image;
   (i) risks.

Some of these overlap and some will apply in combination but the second group of objectives, which may be ancillary to the foregoing include for example:

   (a) training;
   (b) development;
   (c) promotion and succession;
   (d) staff turnover;
   (e) staff changes;
   (f) up or down grading of work;
   (g) restructuring.

Objectives are not equally important and the manager should consider whether these headings are relevant in his own function and to order or rank them in order of priority so that he and his subordinates devote their major efforts and skills to achieving the most valuable results and importance. It is not easy to give a comprehensive set of example objectives because in every area the circumstances will be different. It is suggested, however, that it will be easiest in the first instance if the objectives are listed and four additional columns are drawn in beside them. An example of this is given in Fig. 5.1.

Objectives
The first column lists the objectives which must, whichever heading they are under, be specific, achievable and, of course, desirable. Under some headings such as company image, it may be difficult to be specific, but there is still good reason to attempt this. Such as, for example, the proportion of people knowing the name of the company, or number of disparaging complaints received in a given period.

Action to be taken
In the second column will be put the means of the proposed plan for achieving the objective. In the case of the example of the company image, this may result in redesigning the letter head, or altering the layout of the shop window or spending £1,000 on advertising in the trade press or whatever.

Responsibility of
In column three the actual person who is responsible for carrying out the action specified in the previous column is entered. In many cases this may be yourself; in other cases it would be somebody under your control.

Controls
This column indicates the means by which you will know when you have achieved or are in the process of achieving your objective. For example, how does one know when one's company image has improved to the extent that 10 per cent of the population know the name of the company or that 5 per cent know the name of the company and what it makes? In that rather unusual case perhaps one would be carrying out a sample investigation of the population at large at three-monthly intervals, and then this reveals the appropriate level of recall, then the initial objective would have been achieved.

Objective	Action to be taken	Responsibility of	Controls	Review date
(examples) 1 To select and train deputy by 3.7.80	Prepare job and man specifications. Ask personnel dept. to advertise internally and externally. Ensure John Smith applies.	Manager	Advertisements placed. First interviews Final selection Man in post Training completed.	14.11.79 6.1.80 1.2.80 3.4.80 3.7.80
2 To increase turnover by 15% by 31.12.79	Circulate 100 largest customers once a month drawing attention to best buys and follow by phone calls within 3 days.	Manager – 2 senior sales assistants.	Letters to be posted by end of first week in month	8.7.79 5.8.79 2.9.79
			Review turnover in 3 months to see if increase obtained. Replan if results not satisfactory.	23.9.79
3 To reduce invoicing errors to not more than 5 per month by November 1979.	Record errors daily and post on wall chart.	Senior asst.	Examine chart every Friday and discuss with staff. Review progress.	31.10.79
	Carry out 10% spot check on invoice calculations.	Senior asst.	Reduce to 5% when objective achieved. Review 3 months later.	31.10.79
	Train junior invoice clerk in procedures.	Manager	Junior clerk to be proficient by	29.7.79
	Ask O & M dept. to suggest a clearer invoice layout, and advise on an additional calculator.	Manager	Proposals to be received by	29.7.79

Fig. 5.1 Objectives action plan (specimen)

Review date
The fifth column is either the date by which you wish to have achieved the objective, or the date at which you apply the examination or the controls to see what progress has been made before determining a further control or review date.

Systematic and disciplined approach
Much of this type of exercise is done unconsciously by managers in their everyday life. However, as we have seen before, a systematic and disciplined approach not only covers areas which have been missed but also areas which otherwise would have been swept under the carpet because they are difficult to deal with. If the manager gets into the habit of thinking of his personal and his departmental objectives in specific terms and in concrete dates and plans for achieving them, then he will begin to achieve considerably more and achieving it in a more reliable, satisfying, comprehensive way.

Exercises

1 List three objectives under different headings for your own area, and rank them in order of importance.
2 Prepare an objectives action plan to deal with those three objectives.
3 Consider if there are any of the items on the list of standards which are in no way applicable to your function and state why.

Part II

Managing others

6 Planning and scheduling

'A plan is a list of actions arranged in whatever sequence is thought likely to achieve an objective.'

John Argenti

Providing a service

Whether your function is one of the major areas of direct action such as sales, production and accounts, or a supporting role such as personnel or records, you will be providing a service. The service may be to customers or other outside organisations, or it may be to other internal departments, but whichever it is your job and prospects depend on it being performed in an efficient, competent, and acceptable manner.

Your job is to make a sufficiently good estimate of the likely demands on your department or branch so that you can arrange to have the manpower, materials, equipment and other facilities available to meet these requirements. This chapter looks at some simple methods of forecasting or estimating the likely incidence of demand, and of adjusting manpower resources to meet those peaks and troughs.

When one is attempting to forecast the behaviour of football teams in order to do the Pools, the first step which one takes is to pull out one's 'bankers'. Bankers are teams which are likely to win or likely to lose and if these are entered on the coupon it reduces the number of teams left which have to be considered in detail. The same applies in planning. There are certain things which are known, such as the weekly payroll – it happens every week; other things are known, for example, that Christmas will be on 25 December every year. These are perhaps very simple examples but there are certain things in every business which can be known very well in advance.

Sequence and timing of operations

Planning and scheduling are concerned with the sequence and timing of operations. This will range from 'deciding the priorities' to the batching and allocating of specific parcels of work to be done to a timetable. The information the manager needs will likewise range from the very general, such as a general feeling as to how long one can leave an item before trouble may arise, to detailed work contents of individual procedures, estimates or counts of volumes, timetables of requirements by other departments, customers, and data processing, and plans of staff availability and commitments such as holidays, day-release and courses.

Listing the work

Let us start by listing the work in our particular area. This will be variable, but it will include all the activities performed, e.g. booking orders, processing claims, logging works orders, filing copy letters, training, personnel activities, maintenance, inventories and so on, depending on your function.

Applying two concepts

The second step is to apply two concepts to these specific items of work that we have pulled out.

Concept one

One is that of splitting work up into three distinct parts. Firstly, preparation or make-ready; secondly, the job or operation itself;

and thirdly, the completion phase which may be putting it away or following up afterwards. Let us give an example concerned with a meeting. The preparation phase is the issue of invitations, circulation of agenda and papers, arranging the room and administration, and any briefing activities. The second, or operation phase, is the actual meeting, and the completion phase is the preparation and circulation of minutes, review of action to be taken, filing away the papers, etc.

Over and over again this three-stage concept applies. We get out pen and paper, we write, then put away the pen and paper. We set the table and prepare a meal, we eat it, then we wash up and put away the dishes and cutlery. Within each sequence are others, as when washing-up we get the dirty things, fill the sink, get the washing-up liquid as a preparation phase, then we actually wash up, which is followed by the completion phase of emptying the sink, drying up, and putting away.

Concept two
The second concept which we can apply is to divide the work into three other categories. Firstly, controllable or fixed work; secondly, semi-controllable or semi-fixed work; and thirdly, variable or uncontrollable work. By uncontrollable or controllable the degree of freedom we have over its sequence and timing is meant. For example, the entry of customers into a branch is bound to be variable or uncontrollable in our definition. When we have done this separation, we will find some work which comes in or falls to be done every day, week, month or year whether we like it or not, and that there is some work which comes in in a more sporadic and unexpected way. However, the latter work we can divide into preparation, operation and completion, and in some cases the preparation can be done at our own discretion and the completion can also be done when it is convenient to do it.

You will see that by doing this *we are isolating our 'bankers'*, to use the example quoted earlier – the things which we know, the things which we can control, leaving at the bottom of the list those things which we do not know and therefore cannot control. The proportion of the variable work compared to the rest will vary from business to business, but let us say, for the sake of argument, that it is 50 per cent. In other words, half of the work is comprised of routine or expected work which is subject to normal managerial controls and a certain amount of discretion. The other half is dependent on external influences, e.g. the weather, the political and economic situation, etc. This 50 per cent of variable work can then be subdivided into the three categories of preparation, job and completion and a further proportion of it can therefore be regarded as controllable. One is gradually narrowing down the amount of work to which estimating procedures need to be applied. The best way of estimating the future is to know what has happened in the past: the method of doing this is going to vary from business to business but these notes are suggesting some simple types of planning and scheduling frameworks which may be of assistance.

Simple types of framework

Volume of input

A typical startpoint might be to assess the likely volume of input to the department (e.g. orders, enquiries, etc.). This can be recorded over a period to enable an estimate of the future to be reached, or it may be an informed guess based on knowledge of the business or the plans of other departments. A simple presentation might be as shown in Fig. 6.1.

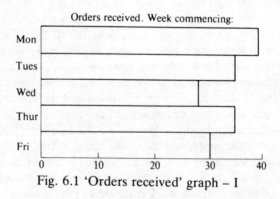

Fig. 6.1 'Orders received' graph – I

Another way is to try putting the graph the other way round and note the difference as shown in Fig. 6.2.

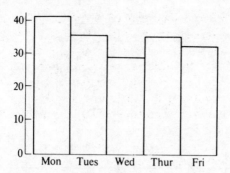

Fig. 6.2 'Orders received' graph – II

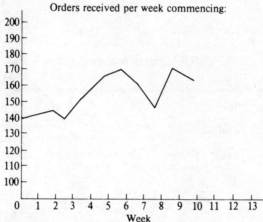

Fig. 6.3 'Orders received' graph – III

Conclusions could be drawn from this pattern; but let us look at another situation in Fig. 6.3

Which is it easier to estimate the future pattern from Fig. 6.3 or Fig. 6.4? The figures are the same in each case.

But consider the first example with a different scale as shown in Fig. 6.5.

Again, the same figures, but it is easier to read.

Moving averages

Another way is to use 'moving averages'. Most volumes and frequencies fluctuate and it may be better to graph the average of the orders of the last four weeks (or last three months etc.) each week to

Orders per week

Week	No.
1	140
2	145
3	150
4	155
5	165
6	157
7	162
8	146
9	170
10	164

Fig. 6.4 'Orders received' graph – IV

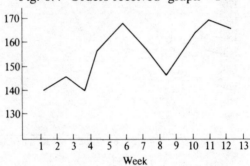

Fig. 6.5 'Orders received' graph – V

get a more reliable picture of the trend. For example as shown in Fig. 6.6.

Would you have made the same forecast from each of the last two graphs? Figures can be made to prove anything, and it is important to look at your method of forecasting to see that it is the most appropriate one to show the pattern of business.

The longer a graph or tabulation is kept, as a general rule, the more reliably one can forecast from it. To offer again a simple example see Fig. 6.7.

On this particular example one could plot in, perhaps as a dotted or coloured line, the forecast for the year, and then continue to plot the actual figures, seeing whether they are as expected, or if not

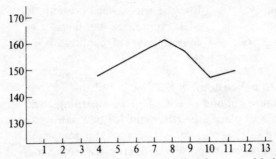

Fig. 6.6 Average orders per week on a moving four-weekly basis – I

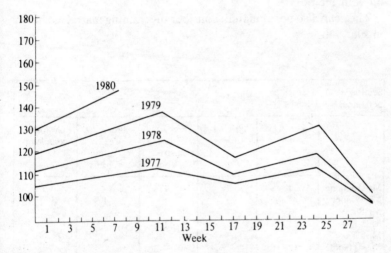

Fig. 6.7 Average orders per week on a moving four-weekly basis – II

whether some of the assumptions one made have changed, and what the implications may be in this and other respects.

Events or tasks

Another type of planning is not concerned with volumes or frequencies, it may relate to events or tasks, e.g.

| 21 December | Christmas lunch |
| 5 January | Children's party |

6 January   Long-service award presentation
9 January   Staff committee meeting
12 January   Sales managers' conference

                        or

Write to old customers X, Y & Z Ltd.
Investigate volume of complaints concerning packaging.
Design and place advertisement for new sales assistant.
Prepare sales report for Mr A. (by 31st January).
Arrange for car to be serviced – replace front shock-absorbers.

Simple schedules of this kind can be diarised, or noted in a
brought-forward file which can be consulted every day (never rely
on your memory!).

They can also be tabulated: consider the training matrix as shown
in Fig. 6.8.

Section personnel	Section tasks				
	Vetting orders	Pricing orders	Preparing works instructions	Preparing weekly sales figures	Customer complaints
Mr Goodone	T	T	T		T
Mr Winner	T	T		T	
Mr Sitter	T	T			
Miss Fitt			T		
Miss Take		T			
Miss Handle					

Fig. 6.8 Training Matrix

Here 'T' indicates that the person concerned is trained or experienced in the function specified. It would show what cover there is
for sickness and holidays, or what would happen if staff leave or are
transferred, or again how the section might be able to cope with
increases of work in one area or another.

A chart like this can be turned into a training plan by deciding
who needs to be trained or cross-trained in what and writing down a
sequence of training to be taken up on a programmed basis, or
whenever the workload drops.

Time	Mr A	Miss B	Miss C
9	Read management figures	Open mail	File yesterday's copies
10	Attend management meeting	Take minutes	Obtain files for day
11	Read mail	Draft minutes	Calculate weekly sales figures
12	Dictate answers	Receive dictation	
1	LUNCH	LUNCH	LUNCH
2	Check minutes	Type letters	Check and type figures
3	Draft	Type letters	Duplicate copies
4	Check and sign	Type minutes	Mark copies for distribution
5	Interview new employee	Prepare outgoing post	Distribute copies

Fig. 6.9 Multiple activity chart – I

Multiple activity chart

Much of the foregoing can be used in a fairly general way but for more detailed planning or scheduling a multiple activity chart may be the answer. Two examples with different degrees of details are shown in Figs. 6.8 and 6.9 for illustration of this.

These particular charts are very simple and show little more than the sequence of operations and interaction of persons. The work will vary each day, so the time blocks are determined by the latest completion points for each activity. Given an assessment of the work content then this can be done more precisely.

	Monday		Tuesday		Wednesday	
Staff	Present	Tasks	Present	Tasks	Present	Tasks
Mr A	X	Budget return	X	Check stocks of sales literature	X	Reorganise window display
		Figures for prize points scheme		Lunch with Sales Manager M N O Ltd.		
Miss B	X	Prepare envelopes from customer mailing list.	X	Complete envelopes		(Dentist a.m.) Prepare payroll
Miss C	(Day off)	—	X	Stamp brochures	X	Sort out stationery cupboard

Fig. 6.10 Multiple activity chart – II

Job	Basis of assessment	Time (mins)	No. Current	No. backlog	Workload
Vetting orders	per 20 orders	30	60	20	2 hours
Pricing orders	per 20 orders	60	40	180	11 hours
Works instructions	per set	10	36	—	6 hours
Sales figures	per set	420	—	—	—
Customer complaints	per each	16	24	93	31¼ hours

Fig. 6.11 Loading chart – I

Job	Basis of assessment	Time (mins)	No. est.	act.	No. b'log	Workload hrs.	mins
Counter tour bookings	This time last year + 10%	25	14			5	50
Written tour bookings	This time last year + 10%	10	2		4	1	00
Counter tour enquiries	2 enquiries per booking (current experience)	7	28			2	16
Written tour enquiries and brochure requests	Last year + 15%	15	4		8	3	00
Rail ticket sales and enquiries	Per 10 tickets sold	90	50			7	30
Business house work	Estimated	180	—			3	00
Customer complaints	6 per day	20	6			2	00
Payroll preparation	Constant	60	1			1	00
Addressing envelopes	Per 15 addressed	60	100			6	40

Fig. 6.12 Loading chart – II

Sample loading charts

The times given in Fig. 6.11 and Fig. 6.12 are for example only.

The load can be programmed into the multiple activity chart or on to a loading table.

Loading table

It may be questioned as to whether, in a small section, it is worth going to this detail or whether an exercise of this type should be done regularly. This is a matter for individual managers, but it should always be considered as a factual proposition. Is 15-30 minutes a day spent on detailed planning by the manager worth a, say, 10 per cent increase in effectiveness (3 persons × 10% of 7 hours = 2.1 hours a day), and will he be able to ensure a more efficient and reliable operation by doing it? Figs. 6.13 and 6.14 show examples of loading tables.

Day	Miss D			Miss E			Miss F		
	Work in	Load hours	Work done	Work in	Load hours	Work done	Work in	Load hours	Work out
Typing itineraries	100	5		100	5				
		4	20		4	20			
		$3\frac{1}{2}$	10		3	20			
		2	30		2	20			
	40	4		30	$3\frac{1}{2}$				
Typing invoices				30	$4\frac{1}{2}$		180	6	
								2	120
									60

Fig. 6.13 Loading table – I

Day	Miss D			Miss E			Miss F		
	Batches in	Load hours	Batches out	Batches in	Load hours	Batches out	Batches in	Load hours	Batches out
Vetting orders	10	5		10	5				
		4	2		4	2			
		3½	1		3	2			
		2	3		2	2			
	4	4		3	3½				
Pricing orders				1	4½		6	6	
								2	4
								—	2

Fig. 6.14 Loading table – II

Tables of this sort can be extended of course to show the position of the work, and of the staff at any time; they can be used to plan the work and its completion, and schedule its performance amongst the staff. This method can be taken further to see how expected rather than actual workloads could be catered for, when work would be completed and when problems of over, or underloading and specialist cover would arise.

Managing peak loads

The principles of managing peak loads are shown in diagrammatic form on pages 54 and 55.

Managing peak loads

The condition

When the capacity to handle work is less than the workload in a period
there is a peak load.

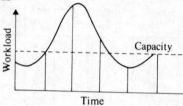

There is a shortfall between the time available to do the work and the
time required to do it.

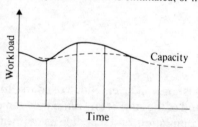

The aim

We have to manage (i.e. set objectives, plan, organise, control, motivate
and innovate) so that the peak condition is eliminated, or much reduced.

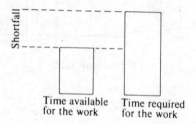

We have to find ways to minimise the shortfall between time available
and time required.

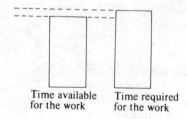

The options

The things we can do to balance work capacity and workload in the peak period fall into three groups.

    1 Increase the time available:

(a) work shifts on machines;

(b) work overtime;

(c) employ temporary staff;

(d) combine two sections;

(e) postpone routine servicing of equipment;

(f) reduce interruptions, e.g. queries.

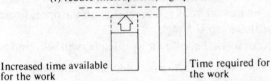

Increased time available for the work   Time required for the work

    2 Decrease the time required for the work:

(a) simplify methods;

(b) motivate – ask for extra effort;

(c) temporarily eliminate some steps, e.g. checks;

(d) temporarily reorganise duties/layout, e.g. flowline;

(e) borrow/hire extra equipment;

(f) install more efficient machines.

    3 Decrease the work to be done:

(a) select priorities – delay non-urgent work;

(b) reschedule work inflow;

(c) send work out;

(d) perform 'make ready' steps in advance.

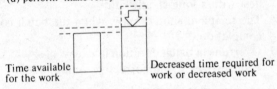

Time available for the work   Decreased time required for work or decreased work

The effect of such actions is to reduce the peak by:

(a) cutting off its top;

(b) taking from its base.

Minimise the peaks' effect by increasing the capacity to handle work.

The solution

Each peak load problem can be solved with a positive approach which draws from the options.

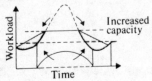

Batching of work

The principles of obtaining higher performance through batching of work are now discussed.

Issuing work in 'batches' facilitates control, particularly where specific deadlines have to be met. A reasonable run at an activity is more satisfying to employees and, if they are allowed to concentrate, they work up to a much higher speed. The 'preparation' and 'completion' phases are reduced in relation to the operation and the employee settles in to the task.

In batching of work the following principles will be found helpful:

1 Batches should, where possible, start and finish with the natural breaks in the working day.
2 Batches should be of the same or similar type of work suited to the skill level of the recipient.
3 Where possible batches should be alternated to provide variety.
4 As a rule the smaller the batch the more sensitive is the control of the situation, but batches less than 10–15 minutes are too small.
5 Batches should be sized according to the preference of the recipient; some people prefer fairly short batches, others work best with a long steady run.
6 The recipient should know when the batch issued is due for completion.
7 Overruns in batch duration in excess of say 15 per cent should be investigated and corrective action taken.

Remember that reasonable pressure of work is good for morale and motivation. Very large amounts of work tend to overwhelm and demoralise staff, but very small quantities may be ignored until the last minute unless there is good feedback and control. By scheduling an objective or plan, can be understood by all in terms of direct action, and by scheduling, good organisation and allocation of work is achieved.

Exercises

1   List the functions or activities of your department.

2   Are there any major figures or incidents which determine the
    level of activity? Can the volume and occurrence of these be
    estimated or are there any historical records to suggest a pat-
    tern?
3   Have you any method of work measurement/assessment? If not,
    how do you work out the correct staffing for present and future
    loads.
4   Are there any activities to which the following techniques could
    be applied?

    (a)   Graphical records or tabulations of quantities.
    (b)   Diary type planning.
    (c)   Matrix planning.
    (d)   Multiple activity charting.
    (e)   Loading charts.
    (f)   Batching controls.
5   Isolate your peaks and troughs and consider whether you could
    use any of the suggestions on p. 55.
6   Construct a training matrix or grid for your department.

7 The decision-making process

'Yet a little sleep, a little slumber – so shall thy poverty come.'
Proverbs XXV

Introduction

All our working life we are concerned with making decisions. Even at a very early stage we are involved in them, e.g. whether it is deciding how to approach the boss; whether to do A before B; whether to try and sell a customer the £60 set or the £80 set; whether to take his cheque or insist on cash; or whether to apply for a vacancy. Right up the tree, the chairman of a large company is still making decisions, e.g. whether to buy another company, whether to proceed into a new market or whether to clinch a deal or not.

At home, again there is a series of big decisions, e.g. whether to have another child; whether to change the car, or whether to buy a bigger house, and small decisions like shall we decorate the toilet this week or shall we leave it till next year, shall we plant onions again this year when they did so badly last year, or shall we go for some more potatoes?

Decisiveness

All these decisions have one thing in common and that is that we are never in possession of all the facts on which to evaluate them thoroughly, in other words to prove the point. If we were able to prove the point completely, then perhaps the need for making the decision would be of a different quality. However, when we are not able to 'prove the point', but must make a decision on a balance of probabilities or estimates or guesses, then we are very much dependent on another quality which is decisiveness. This is the capacity to make up our minds and decide to take action, and then to take that action, when we are not in possession of all the facts.

At one end of the spectrum we will have people who will make a decision, take action, in possession of no facts at all, or practically no facts – we would call these people reckless. At the other end of the spectrum we have people who will carry on calling for further facts and doing further investigations without reaching a decision at all. Or there are those people who keep changing their mind. I am sure all of us have worked with people who come to a conclusion one day, and then rethink the thing or the matter again the following day, and come to a different conclusion. Who is to say they are 'wrong', but then action, which is the lifeblood of business, is not taken perhaps when it should be. In addition, the staff who have been looking to us for a lead find it very frustrating if we keep changing our minds. If they have to adjust to new policies too frequently, they come to the conclusion that perhaps we do not know what we are doing.

I am sure you will have all deduced by now that decisiveness comes with confidence, and confidence comes with knowing what we are doing, or at least thinking that we are knowing what we are doing.

In this chapter we are offering a simple system for discipling the mind – the subject of decision-making – and also one or two techniques for assisting in evaluating one course of action opposed to another.

Mechanics of decision making

This is illustrated in Fig. 7.1 and consists of the following:

Define problem
Examine facts
Consider alternatives
Include views of others
Decide course of action
Evaluate results

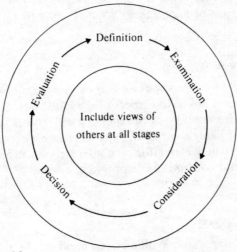

Define the problem

This is so obvious that it hardly needs saying, and because it is hardly
ever said, it is frequently overlooked. By defining the problem one
often defines the answer. A manager, pestered by a lot of simple
questions from his staff, got them to put them in writing. Much to his
surprise he found that many were never brought to him because in
defining the query sufficiently to write it, the answer became apparent. Problems are often expressed in vague terms, e.g. 'massive
inflation', 'ecological suicide', 'planning blight', etc., which have
emotive overtones, and suggest a disaster situation. Since the situation is a disaster 'there is nothing we can do about it' and the
decision process moves away from solving the problem to avoiding
it, whether to commit suicide, get drunk, or emigrate. However, if
we know we must budget for, say, a 25 per cent increase in costs, or
that we have fifty years left to develop an alternative to fossil fuels,
then we have defined the problem better, and in doing so pointed to
the action to be taken to solve the problem.

A problem often encountered is 'we need more sales' (or, presumably to make more profit from existing business), but how much

more sales? If the problem can be defined, e.g. to make the required return we need £x more income, then we can start to consider how those sales can be secured. It may be that £y more of a product or service needs to be sold, or whatever, but you are in a better position to start the decision-making process. Always be clear on what the problem is as exactly as you can before you start on any decision-making process of importance. What is really the matter?

Examine the facts

Let us write down what facts we know about the problem and what facts we do not know. In respect of the latter facts let us consider how much effort or how much expense it will require to obtain these facts, and the likely accuracy of these facts once we obtain them. We can go to a great deal of effort to obtain facts which are of doubtful validity to our solution of the problem.

Consider alternatives

This is very important. With an open mind we should consider all the possible courses of action which could be taken. Many people who have let their minds wander, either a personal brainstorm, or a brainstorming session which can be conducted with others, and have thought of 'stupid' alternative ways of doing things, have stumbled on quite important ways of doing things to better advantage.

Include the views of others

This is noted here as the fourth step because it fits the fourth letter of the mnemonic 'DECIDE'. However, it is an ancillary to all other steps in the decision process. Including the views of others is important for two reasons. One, because others may think of ideas which you have not thought of yourself, or may be in possession of information which you do not already have. The other reason is that if your staff feel that they have participated in decisions they will be more readily willing to identify themselves with the action that has to be taken as a result.

Decide the course of action

The decision is made by balancing quantified advantages and profits, and unquantified advantages and benefits, against quantified costs and disadvantages, against unquantified costs and disadvantages. Obviously, the closer these are to each other then the more difficult the decision will be to make. Some methods of evaluation are offered later in this chapter.

Evaluate results

If we have made the right decision, justified by subsequent events, we should consider why it was we made that right decision and whether the same line of thinking or line of action would lead to us making the right decision again. If we have made the wrong decision, have we made the wrong decision for the right reasons, or have we made the wrong decision because we have pursued an unsatisfactory decision-making process, or have we been lacking certain important facts? Unless we do this evaluation after our decisions, then we may in fact find ourselves making the same mistake over and over again, or perhaps even worse, making the right decision several times and then making a disastrous mistake because we are not aware exactly of what we are doing.

Factors in evaluation

Ranking

This is the simplest form of evaluation in which we decide that x is better than y and y is better than z, and so we can set out our list of alternatives or list of priorities in order of importance.

Weighting

This is a step further than ranking, in which we say that x is equal to 10, y is equal to 5 and c is equal to nought etc. In other words, some factors have more importance than others. Let us give an example of this. We are to choose a branch manager for an insurance company and we decide that we are going to make our choice on five factors: technical knowledge, managerial skill, personal relations, maturity and seniority. We decide technical knowledge of the business is most important and give it a value of 10; managerial skill is important but less important than insurance knowledge, so we give it a factor of 7; personal relations are very important but not quite so important as the others, so we give it a factor of 6; seniority is important in our company, and we give it a factor of 3; maturity is similar to seniority but slightly more important and we rank it as 4. (See Table 7.1.)

You will see now that we have ranked the various qualities which we think a manager of our particular branch should have, but we have gone one stage further and we have applied weightings to them because some characteristics are more important than others. These particular weightings and rankings may not be applicable in your company, but they are given as examples.

The next step in using these factors is to add all the factors together and you will see that in this case it comes to the total of 30. We would then divide each particular factor, for example 10 for insurance knowledge, by 30 and come out with a decimal result. In the case of insurance knowledge ·333, managerial skill ·233, personal relations, ·200, maturity ·133, and seniority ·100.

Finally, the various applicants are interviewed for the branch manager's position and each one is rated against the various factors which you have chosen on the score from 1 to 10. At the end of the interviews we then multiply the various scores for each man or woman as the case may be, by the decimal factor and we complete with a weighted score or corrected score for each person interviewed. This will not automatically make the choice for us of our new branch manager, but it will lead us to making a better quality decision through thinking about the subject in a disciplined way, and where the choice between one man and another is narrow, it will help us to make the decision on a more rational basis.

Desirability and probability

Not all decisions have the same effects. It is very important for us to pick the right branch manager to continue our example, but if we have picked the wrong man, there are a number of actions we can take to mitigate the effects of our bad decision. We can dismiss him, we can transfer him, we can train him or supervise him. So there we have a very important but not an irrevocable decision.

If we back a horse in a race for £1 we are making a different kind

Table 7.1 Specimen table showing use of weighting

Rank	Quality	Weight	Factor wt. ÷ by total of wts.	Candidate A		Candidate B		Candidate C	
				Eval. (raw score) out of 10	Weighted score (raw score X factor)	Raw score	Weighted score	Raw score	Weighted score
1	Insurance knowledge	10	·333	6	2·000	9	3·000	4	1·332
2	Managerial skill	7	·233	7	1·631	5	1·165	7	1·631
3	Personal relations	6	·200	7	1·400	5	1·000	10	2·000
4	Maturity	4	·133	9	1·200	8	1·065	10	1·330
5	Seniority	3	·100	8	·800	10	1·000	6	·600
		30	1·000	37	7·031	37	7·230	37	6·893

of decision because once the bet has been placed it cannot be cancelled – the horse either wins or loses. If we are a little less decisive, we back it for a place. But once the race has been won or lost, there is nothing we can do about the result.

If we lose £1 by backing the wrong horse, it is not a terribly important thing, but had we been backing with a month's wages, for example, then the decision would lead to certain tensions inside us and it would be an important irrevocable decision. If we had such a decision to make we would probably shrink from making it. The probability of a horse winning would have to be very high for us to take such a risk.

This introduces the question of desirability and probability. The desirability of our having a big win on a race track is very high; the probability of our doing so in that particular case is low.

In our earlier step of defining the problem, we have probably decided what are the desirable characteristics in a successful decision on the particular point on which we are engaged. In many business decisions this is profit, and if we apply the probability of certain aspects of our evaluation occurring to the desirability factors, we then have another dimension in our decision-making. Let us take an example.

You are proposing to operate a holiday centre on a certain island in the Mediterranean. You first of all estimate your likely business in this holiday centre, and you would then rank the various possible levels of booking. Let us say that for 1978 these would be 25, 75, 125, 175 and 225 (flights). A big variation, but of course in practice the project could be a great success or fall flat on its face, although you would have some measure of control by the actions you took over whether this was so or not. The next stage is to put a factor of probability against each of those booking levels. This is very similar to the weighting of importance which we applied to the various characteristics which we apply to our branch manager. In the case of probability the maximum probability is 100 per cent. Therefore, one must divide 100 per cent between the various levels of bookings in their probability. Let us say for the sake of this example that we take 12 or ·12 as the likelihood of making up 25 or 225 flights, we get 23 as the probability of 75 and 175, and 30 as the probability of 125. We are saying, in fact, that we are most likely to reach a medium point on the bookings but we are not very certain that that is going to be the case.

Let us set these out (as shown in Table 7.2) and then consider what we should do. On the island there is an existing hotel which is in a poor state of maintenance, and we have the choice of either converting the existing hotel, building a new hotel or, in fact, doing both. There are many considerations to be applied but in terms of profit our accountant has worked out what would happen.

Table 7.2 Example calculation

Bookings on XYZ island – proposed holiday centre

Booking levels	25	75	125	175	225
Probability	·12	·23	·30	·23	·12

Gross profit at booking levels

Alternatives					
1 Convert existing hotel	£350	£1,080	£1,800	£1,800	£1,800
2 Build new hotel	£340	£1,080	£1,800	£2,500	£2,500
3 Do both	£320	£1,050	£1,780	£2,500	£3,200

Profitability converted by probability factors

					Gross expectation
£42	£248	£540	£414	£216	£1,460
£40	£248	£540	£575	£200	£1,603
£39	£242	£534	£575	£384	£1,774

One sees the gross profits likely at each different level of booking, and then by converting the gross profits to probabilities by multiplication with our probability factors, we come to the second set of figures which shows our gross expectation. One will see that at £1,774 we have the greatest potential profit in building the new hotel and in also converting the existing hotel. Again, this kind of mechanism may not make our decision for us, but it will put us in a much better position to evaluate the alternatives than we would otherwise have been in, and it will not have failed your notice that our profit budgeting for that and the following year will be much easier having done a calculation of this kind.

Without the benefit of analytical tools, the human mind tends to make decisions in two ways. A problem occurs and the mind looks at its memory and says, 'where have I met a problem like that before, how was it solved?'; the second thing that it tends to do is to stop once the needle in the haystack has been found, whereas it may be better policy (I only say 'may') to look through the whole of the haystack to see how many more needles there are and then make a choice of the best needle.

Exercises

1   What decisions do you regularly make? List six, and describe what method you use to make them. Are any 'win/lose', i.e. irrevocable decisions?
2   What was the biggest decision you have ever made? How did you make it, and was it successful?
3   List three decisions which could be made by using ranking.
4   List three decisions where simple ranking would be improved by weighting.
5   List three decisions where the use of probabilities would be significant.
6   Have you ever avoided making a decision or felt like avoiding one? Are there any decisions you would avoid now?
7   Are there any circumstances where it is better to stick to a bad decision than to reverse it? Give an example.
8   What factors would contribute most to improved decision-making in your company?

8   Meetings and reports

Definition of a committee: the unqualified drawn from the unwilling to consider the unnecessary.

Meetings

It is sometimes said that the best meeting is a committee of three with two absent. Meetings may be held for the purpose of disseminating or collecting information, or for communicating decisions, but the meeting we are talking about here is where several interested parties sit down and work through an agenda, either planned or spontaneous, discussing each subject in turn and arriving at conclusions for action.

Necessity and purpose

The first thing to do is to decide exactly what the meeting is expected to achieve and whether this is reasonable. Perhaps the next thing is to decide whether to hold the meeting or attend the meeting at all. Time is being spent with a number of managers, and one should consider whether the cost is going to be commensurate with the result. Are we ready to hold a meeting, and are you ready to play your part in it? One cannot be axiomatic about this, but I try never to attend any meeting for which I am not properly prepared or briefed. If one finds oneself discussing unexpected items on the agenda, or one is in areas where one has not done one's homework, valuable time will be wasted in the meeting, and you may find yourself having to adopt a negative approach because you have not done your own thinking in advance.

Therefore, prepare yourself, and make sure that you know what the meeting is for; estimate what you think is its likely result. And, if this is good for you it is good for the other people who should be invited – they must be given an opportunity to read any necessary papers in advance and know what is likely to arise for decision. You would also work out their likely personal objectives and the probable course of their personal approach (and also your own). Consider who can usefully contribute to, and gain from, the meeting, but there are others who should be advised for political or status reasons. Perhaps if you keep them informed they do not actually need to attend.

Before it starts

Get to the meeting before it starts. I do not mean merely be on time (and how much time is wasted by people sitting around waiting for the chairman or other members to arrive?). This is the question of getting used to the surroundings of the meeting, getting your papers laid out, etc., so that you can concentrate fully when the meeting starts. In furtherance of this, the good secretary will see that the administration does not obtrude and that there are sufficient chairs, tables, paper, pencils, etc., and that coffee or tea if appropriate have been ordered.

During the meeting

When the meeting starts the chairman should not assume automatically that all members realise what the meeting is for; he should state clearly what its purpose is. No advantage is gained by making the meeting last any longer than is required for achieving these purposes. The cost of salaries of those attending the meeting can be substantial, and their absence at the meeting often means that departmental and other decisions are delayed until their return. Committees become little groups in their own right and time is spent on matters which have no relation to the objectives of the enterprise.

If you are making proposals, then always explain them in terms of what effect they will have on the others who are listening; consider why they should be interested in listening to what you have to say, if at all. You must draw out and listen to the arguments of others and be patient with objections. Very often people are content to have the opportunity to state an objection, and having blown themselves out, as it were, will allow matters to proceed.

In real life there are very few proposals which receive immediate and unanimous approval, if they have been given any proper consideration. Some suggestions as to how to present proposals in the most favourable light are covered in Chapter 10.

In meetings remember to 'take the temperature'. You should learn to study the expressions on the faces of those around the table and notice what they are doing, e.g. whether they are sitting back with their arms folded in an expression of withdrawal or leaning forward tensed up with something they would perhaps like to say; they may be nodding with approval or frowning with anxiety. If the mood is moving towards acceptance then, of course, a decision can be reached and recorded. If the decision seems to be going against what you want, and if this matters, stop that decision being made. You can easily say that there are more facts or analyses to be done, or that this was a preliminary proposal at this stage or defer it in some other way. Once a 'no' decision has been made it is much more difficult to reverse.

Eventually you will have made your points or proposals and the meeting will be moving to a conclusion. If the conclusion is the one you want this is fine, although one's colleagues do not always like to see too much manifest success. Whatever conclusion the meeting reaches, even if it is to continue the discussion at the next meeting, it should be specifically agreed, and if minutes are taken, recorded before going on to the next item. Where action is determined, it helps to put the name or initials of the person concerned against the minute and to declare some time for review or completion. For example, compare 'it was decided that the production department should review the situation concerning excessive scrap', with 'Mr. Smith, the production director, agreed to submit a report on scrap percentages by 17 May and circulate it to the members of the meeting'.

Reviewing the situation

There should obviously be some mechanism of reviewing action taken on decisions by any meeting and the composition and frequency of the meeting should also be down for review at regular intervals. Many businesses have regular meetings which are little more than a talking shop. Another fact to consider is how long people can concentrate and stay awake at a meeting. There are meetings which go on for hours and hours and everyone concerned feels very heroic when they stagger back to their homes in the late evening. While they have been at the meeting they are either unobtainable in their departments, or else subject to a series of disturbing interruptions during the meeting. A suggestion is to decide how long the meeting should decently take and keep to that so that other arrangements can be planned around the meeting.

Summary

1 Determine the objective of the meeting.
2 Prepare yourself – plan the tactics and timetable.
3 Decide who should attend.
4 Advise the participants in time for them to prepare.
5 Have ready all necessary papers. Circulate to others who need to see them in advance.
6 Arrange accommodation and administrative details.
7 Start the meeting on time.
8 State the purpose(s) of the meeting.
9 Direct the discussion, stage by stage.
10 Take the temperature. Always keep in mind the objectives and feelings of participants.
11 Agree conclusions specifically at each stage.
12 Nominate persons responsible for action and for review.
13 Arrange the time and date of the next meeting (if required).

Reports

In management literature, meetings and reports seem generally to be linked, presumably because very often a report is either called for by a meeting or is presented to a meeting. This may be the best way of dealing with the situation, but the manager will consider whether by calling a meeting of this kind he is 'syndicating' the risk, rather than allowing the person responsible to make the decision on his own.

There are two distinct phases in constructing a report. The first is to marshal all necessary information; the second is to write this information in the way most conducive to the right decision or action being taken.

Marshalling necessary information

As a minimum, you must have answers to these questions:

1 What is the real problem? What specific illustrations can you give of the real problem? What is the report meant to say?
2 What is the answer to the problem? Does the report give the answer or enable the recipient to form a satisfactory conclusion; again, can you provide specific illustrations?
3 Why should the recipient be interested in the answers? What benefits will it provide? Again, be specific in defining the benefits or results. Benefits which cannot be quantified become a matter of subjective opinion.
4 If results and benefits are involved state clearly how much these will cost in various forms of resource and how long it will take to achieve them.

The marshalling exercise consists of writing down every relevant fact, proposal or conclusion, preferably on separate pieces of paper so that these can be sorted into a logical sequence at the second stage.

Framework of the report

In planning the arrangement of a report two approaches can be taken. One is that where there is a standard company form it may be better to follow this as the recipient will be familiar with it. However, where there is no standard form, or where the standard form seems inappropriate, the arrangement should follow a form which satisfies the reader's priority of interest. Normally you state the results first, and then discuss how you arrive at them. A form which normally satisfies this and is widely used is the summary or précis report which covers the following points:

(a) objective or purpose;

(b) scope or summary;
(c) conclusions;
(d) recommendations.

Body of the report

Objective or purpose
The purpose of doing a summary report, which should be seldom
more than two or three pages long, is to orientate the mind of the
reader and to make it possible for those who are not wishing to
question the conclusions to ascertain what they are, without having
to wade through all the supporting details.

Scope or summary
Reports should always have a title and a date and indicate to whom
they are addressed and by whom they were prepared. The report
should contain an index or contents page showing what it contains
and where it can be found. The summary or précis report should
follow; the précis commences with a statement of the objectives of
the report, why it was commissioned, who asked for it and when.
The scope or summary briefly indicates the resources and method
employed so as to give an indication of the depth of the conclusions
and to draw attention to any special features of the work. This,
however, like the previous paragraph, should not be more than two
or three lines in the normal way.

Conclusions
Then should follow the conclusions or findings. This should be done
in tabular form, and in a series of positive statements. For example

(a) that a reduction in wastage of 3 per cent could be obtained by
     . . . ;
(b) that orders could be processed through the office in 24 hours
     if . . . ;
(c) that an additional assistant manager in the export section be
     appointed with effect from . . . ;
(d) that the reason for the accident was the . . . .

Recommendations
The final part of the summary is the recommendations, and this is a

list of specific actions to be taken following on from the conclusions. For example:

    (a) that the factory manager be authorised to obtain tenders for a new grinding machine with the object of having it installed by December 1979;

    (b) that the revised method of order processing be installed by the office manager on 16 May and that the organisation and methods department be requested to assist in the installation;

    (c) that the personnel manager be asked to proceed with the recruitment for the new assistant manager position;

    (d) that the committee's findings be forwarded by the secretary to Mr Bloggs at the Home Office.

Writing the report

Most people have no need to be involved in any systematic writing or literary effort after leaving school or college. It may be, therefore, that the manager who finds himself needing to write a substantial report or letter will find it a difficult exercise. He may make the report too brief and sketchy, or long and tedious, or evade it altogether and try to get by with a verbal proposal. Indeed, a verbal proposal may be a very good way of obtaining approval, but all managers will need to write some important proposal, report or letter at some stage.

Good writing needs a disciplined approach and repeated polishing to be persuasive. Good writing cannot be acquired overnight; it cannot be won through a formula, and it is also unlikely that without regular use the ability will remain at a satisfactory level. There are, however, some guidelines which will give you a better prospect of success. These guidelines are now discussed.

Include testimonials or illustrations in reports

For example: 'similar equipment was installed in the ABC and the XYZ company last year and has given satisfactory performance'. 'This type of training has produced remarkable results in the invoice department. Three operators increased output by 25 per cent within two weeks following the course'. 'The scope for obtaining savings through methods improvements is substantial. As an example the replacement of typed addressing on envelopes by the use of window envelopes has saved 150 hours of typing each month'. 'The problems facing the division cannot be compared too closely with those confronting the other areas of the company. However, in a competitive company MNO Limited, there was a somewhat similar situation when . . . .'

Use linking words in your writing
Linking words help the reader follow your thinking and they are most important in opening paragraphs. Examples of such words are:

next	nor	remaining	yet
besides	so	the result	final
then	also	in contrast	first . . .
alternatively	similarly	in total	second . . .
previously	specifically	in some	third . . .
equally	meanwhile		

Next time you read anything by a successful author or writer see whether these linking words have been used to carry your attention from one point to another.

Headings and sub-headings
Chapter headings and sub-headings attract more readers than the body of the report does. If they are persuasive these lines help sell the reader; if they convey little, they lessen reader interest. The test here is which headline or heading conveys the information most persuasively or clearly. As an example, judge for yourself which heading should go on a paragraph: 'benefits' or 'financial benefits for company staff'. Try this one: 'findings' or 'your principal problem areas'. Short, dry headings, for example, 'distribution report by so and so' may be succinct, but 'opportunities for reducing distribution costs in the XYZ depot' may attract more interest.

March your readers through your sub-headings
That sounds a difficult task, but if you use frequent sub-headings, say every 200 or 250 words, you will flag your readers through their task. They know from the heading what is coming up in the next sentences. These reinforce the sub-heading and, therefore, you make your good points twice over. As with headings, so with subheadings, a single word may count for nothing. 'Resources' conveys

little but 'additional staff resources for the textile division' would surely merit closer attention.

Power words
Some words add power to headlines and sub-headings. Consider using them when appropriate; words such as:

important	advice	remarkable	loss
improvement	how to	announcing	win
quick	introducing	fear	first

Avoid long words, sentences and paragraphs
The jargon words of technical specialists and the ponderous phrases of outback orators tend to drive readers elsewhere. Use short plain English words, and in your first draft write sentences of between ten and twenty words. If you want to add style this should be done at the final drafting of the report. Try to restrict your paragraphs to eight lines or under. Use active verbs to give force and drive to what you have to say. For example, 'we installed a computer' (active) 'the computer was installed by us' (passive).

Cut verbiage
It depends on what you are writing but, as suggested earlier, you should initially write down everything which comprises the work done to produce the report, but as a second stage you should cut out everything that is really not relevant. Such trimming, and many letters and reports could be cut by a third, can rarely be done at the time of the first draft. It comes in the editing or polishing stage. It is very difficult for a writer to edit his own writing as he *knows* what he meant to say. If you can get a colleague to read and comment, he may point out that the sentence that was quite clear to you could convey another meaning to someone else, or it could appear confused. Most people have a rather subjective impression of their own ideas and views, and in any case, if you have spent some time in compiling the report or letter a fresh approach may well be of value.

Go straight to the point
When giving recommendations or conclusions, do not lead into them with a number of lines. Simply state as follows:

The recommendations are:

1 . . . .
2 . . . .
3 . . . .

and the same with any other results or statements. Make your points
quickly and save your readers' time. If you want to expand, do so
after your first enumeration, by saying: 'the following facts support
those recommendations' or 'more detailed information follows'.

Tabulate paragraphs
For a series of unrelated facts or progressive paragraphs, a useful
device is to number them sequentially. Do not string disconnected
thoughts together in long slabs of type.

Use of capitals
DO NOT USE LARGE NUMBERS OF CAPITALS. PEOPLE
READ ALL THEIR BOOKS, NEWSPAPERS AND
MAGAZINES IN LOWER CASE. This applies, also, to the
report's table of contents. The reader's first impression is of
strangeness when a lot of capitals are used. He does not write in
capitals so why should you?

Avoid negatives
The use of negatives confuses and turns what should be simple into
something which is complex. For example, 'this is not to say that
additional training would be unwarranted in all circumstances, nor
that it could not be positively beneficial in certain cases'. The writer
of that complex sentence could have said just as easily 'additional
training may be beneficial in certain cases'.

Avoid bull
Take for example the following statement: 'I am absolutely convinced that the proposals would be the best thing ever for the
department, and the equipment proposed is the most advanced
available in the world today'. This sort of statement over-
emphasises the point and leads to resistance on the part of the
reader; in any case it adds very little to the content of the report.

Avoid stating the obvious

Summarise

This final point is one of the most important of all. Summarise, in
three or four sentences, at the opening of each report, chapter, or
each main section of your letter. Summaries are probably best
written in some distinctive way at the beginning of the section to
which they refer, but you may summarise at the beginning of the
letter or report, at the end of it, or within individual chapters, or in a
covering letter if there is one. You do not want to confuse the reader
by using different literary tricks, but it may be valuable in stressing
what you want to say to summarise at any appropriate point in the
report.

To summarise

1 Use examples, testimonials and illustrations.
2 Use linking words.
3 Pay special attention to headings and sub-headings.
4 March your readers through your sub-headings.
5 Use 'power words'.
6 Avoid long words, long sentences, long paragraphs.
7 Cut verbiage.
8 Go straight to the point.
9 Tabulate paragraphs.
10 Avoid negatives.
11 Avoid bull.
12 Avoid stating the obvious.
13 Summarise.

Exercises

Meetings

1 Prepare an agenda for a meeting at which the various meetings
   held in your organisation will be reviewed. List the meetings
   involved, the attendance and the appropriate duration.
2 Imagine the meeting has taken place and you have had your way
   in all respects. Draft minutes to record the decisions taken.
3 Imagine that the board has decided to relocate in a development
   area 150 miles away. You have to announce this to the senior
   executives at a meeting. Prepare a plan of how to put the

decision over most effectively and consider how you would deal with any likely objections or queries.

Reports and letters

4   Write a newspaper article of 'not more than 500 words' illustrating your present job or project.
5   Examine your last major letter or report and criticise it in the light of the points in this chapter. Would you have written it any differently on reflection, and how?
6   Draft a short report addressed to your chief executive outlining the three weakest aspects of your organisation and proposing the necessary action and restructuring required.
7   Write an application letter for a better position showing why you should be given serious consideration for it.

9 Motivation

'If you are not contributing to the solution of the problem, then you are part of the problem yourself.'

Chinese proverb

Meaning

Let us first of all try to define what we mean by motivation. Consider one situation: you bound up your garden path after work, throw open the front door and give your wife a big hug. 'I had a wonderful day at the office dear, I got so much done,' you say to her. 'I did this, I did that, I got this agreed, I finished that, etc., etc.,' and so you go on all evening telling her about the wonderful events of the day. This goes on until you suddenly realise it is half past ten and you suggest an early night so that you will be fresh for the meeting tomorrow morning. Needless to say you bound out of bed at first light the following day and rush into work with your head full of all your plans.

Contrast an alternative situation: you drag yourself up the front path, fumble with the lock and sink into the big chair. 'Get me a drink, dear,' you gasp, 'and make it a big one, I'm just about all in. I've had a hellish day at the office, I got absolutely nothing done'.

The majority of practising managers live their lives on a more even keel than is demonstrated by those two extremes of feeling, and perhaps it is better that they should do. However, work occupies the major part of waking time and energies as managers and employees for, possibly forty-seven years of our lives, assuming that most people start at about eighteen and retire at about sixty-five years of age. The difference in terms of productivity and creativity, apart from personal values, in living those forty-seven years as a kind of pleasurable and exciting activity or as a drag must be enormous. If the difference were as little as 10 per cent, and most experienced managers will know that it is considerably greater than this, it would be the equivalent of working another five years during one's career.

Different approaches

The manager has to decide how motivated he wants his employees to be. There may be some occupations where a relatively static frame of mind is better because there is little demand or opportunity in the position. Certain security and reception positions might fall into this category. This chapter suggests a number of approaches which can be tried in order to stimulate the phagocytes of your idle and apathetic subordinates.

Basic points
First of all, here are some basic points.

Children
When we are young we are very dependent on others, e.g. our parents. If those others satisfy the child's needs and make him feel secure and loved, then when he grows up his attitudes are more likely to be secure and dependent, socially inclined and to be associated with people, because he is used to people satisfying his needs.

If a child does not know where he stands and cannot exert influence over his environment he will become insecure (fearful), aggressive (hostile), and will seek independence. He will concentrate on personal (egotistic) needs, with ways and means by which he can obtain the independence he desires, e.g. power, control, money and the acquisition of material things.

If the child wants independence and cannot get it he will retreat into fantasy. If you (child) do not get what you want you react with aggression. How do the parents react? Submit or attack back? Probably they get the child to repress his aggressive feelings, so there is often tumult under a calm exterior.

In fact we do suppress our feelings and our outward appearance may not reflect what is happening inside – and what happens inside is different for different people – not everyone views the world from the same perspective, or the same perspective as you.

People we know

When we 'know' people well, such as relatives or close friends, we do not always understand exactly what happens inside their minds, but we know pretty well how they will behave in a variety of situations. We know how they will react to what we say and do, because we have seen them reacting in the past. This applies also to groups of people we have come to know, i.e. the customers, the staff, head office, XYZ Ltd., etc., and this is fine, so long as we do not assume that because people are behaving in a particular way, they have a similar feeling about what they are doing and why they are doing it.

People we do not know so well

The problem arises when dealing with people one does not know so well, such as new customers or new members of staff, or where a novel situation arises, or where people start to react in an unexpected or contradictory way. It is in dealing with such situations that the manager proves himself, but first of all he must start by understanding himself.

Let us take an example. The owner of your company, Mr Smith, has been trying to get the business of a certain large firm for years. He seems at last to be succeeding and has been asked to meet its managing director next Tuesday afternoon at 4.00 p.m. He asks you to accompany him and to prepare a write-up on the company to be used at the meeting. This seems to be recognition for you, and naturally you want to do well at the meeting – particularly as you are an assistant branch manager and one of the managers at another branch may be leaving shortly.

You work all weekend, and with the help of your own manager

you produce a marvellous folder and write-up to bring to the meeting. You are to meet Mr Smith outside the customer's premises just before the appointed time. Naturally you arrive early, at 3.30 p.m. and wait. At 4.00 p.m. he has not arrived, so you go into reception; he is not there, and eventually you decide to go in to the call yourself. However, the receptionist tells you that there is no appointment arranged for Mr Smith or yourself; she allows you to telephone back to your company, but Mr Smith's secretary says that he went on a visit to Tenerife two days ago and didn't he tell you?

Reactions
How do you feel at that juncture, how do you react to the situation? Three types of reactions are possible:

1 Angry – directed against Mr Smith or more generalised disgust with the company, job, etc.
2 Disappointed – humiliated. Do you feel ashamed or cast down in yourself?
3 Rational, e.g. I wonder why he didn't tell me? What should I do next? etc.

Most people would feel some of each type of reaction, but we can be reasonably predictive about which would predominate.

Mr A has been successful at school and in his private life; he did well in his last job and he has good and easy relationships within the company. Mr B has not found life so easy and has just scraped through. He is not well known in the company and has had some uneasy encounters in his time.

How will A and B react? Self-confident A will be surprised and frustrated by this check to his progress and will probably be angry with the obstacle and those responsible for it. B, pessimistic about his abilities but who would nevertheless like to be successful, may react differently. He may vent his anger inwardly – perhaps as a further proof of his own inadequacy or his stupidity in taking on the job or task. In other words a series of failures brings a man to the conclusion that he can be no longer certain that the world has gone wrong – perhaps it is himself that is lacking – and of course vice versa.

The third reaction – the purely rational one – is more rare. He is the man who feels no emotional upset at all, any more than dropping a coin on the floor or forgetting his handkerchief. It is a problem, but not worth getting excited about. How does the perspective of Mr C differ from A or B? I am not talking here of apparent reactions, but real reactions. It is a situation in which A and B's needs for status and self-esteem are challenged. Mr C lives in a wider and more secure world in which his esteem needs have been satisfied many times and he can see a variety of methods of achieving his aims, and, possibly, a variety of aims. Both A and B could mature into C – but as and if they do, they will be less likely to encounter obstacles that seem serious (for them), and will be less likely to blow up if they encounter them.

However, in business life, if one does meet an obstacle which leads to very angry feelings, it is bad form to get very angry about it. You show a controlled and rational façade. Inside your blood pressure is rising, and there may well be physical side effects in due course. (An occasional blow-off would be a healthy thing.)

The ideal executive is the one who does not get frustrated in the first place, i.e. Mr C, who simply shrugs his shoulders at himself and the world and starts to think where to go from there. His self-esteem is so solid that few things could threaten it. His ego-needs are for accomplishment of organisational goals – achievement and self-actualisation.

People's expectations
What is the problem? It is of people's expectations about their ability to satisfy their needs, and their expectations effectively determined by past successes and failures.

If, through life, one has come to expect failure and feel unsure of one's ability to satisfy one's personal egoistic needs, then these needs loom larger than they do for the next man. The American psychologist H. J. Leavitt gives an example of a badly mixed drink: is it just a badly mixed drink or a sign of disrespect from the barman?

People like Mr B will be less rational about their efforts to satisfy their needs – it follows that one should build up people's feelings of self confidence. Let us turn to success and failure since experience of both has such a major effect.

Success and failure
Mrs A and Mrs B are of equal ability. Mrs B thinks a salary of £2,000 p.a. means success, while Mrs A thinks £3,000 p.a. means

making money. Both earn £2,500 p.a. but which thinks she is a failure?

There is a relationship between our aspirations and our ability to achieve them. The closer they are the better; excess either way creates frustration. People develop different attitudes, even from an early age. Take an example. As a counter clerk you are on an incentive scheme. The first month of the scheme your sales are £4,000. You have worked hard but you aim for £5,000 sales the following month. In most situations in life we tend to set goals slightly ahead of our present abilities or performance. But suppose another counter clerk, younger than you, gets a result of £6,500 sales in the month. What is your target then, and how would you feel about selling only £5,000 when you try?

Once other people enter into the target-setting process the more or less natural tendency to set targets a little ahead, or related to, past achievement breaks down. Targets may be set without any regard to ability. In business or industrial life standards are accepted or imposed which are inappropriate to the individual's inclinations or abilities, resulting in frustration (or refusal to accept). Frustration arises where failure to surmount an obstacle threatens one's personal well-being.

Self-confidence is tied to success, and success is in large part what other people may decide it is.

Conflict of goals
Another problem is where goals conflict with each other, e.g. needs for dependence and independence. Particularly where the conflict relates to internal conscience needs. Remember that repressing feelings burns up a lot of energy.

Take an example. You are assistant to Mr X – a very decent hard-working man. He has helped you a lot and you are good friends. He has been in the position a long time and is desperately wanting promotion. He has a large family and has a bit of a struggle to make ends meet. The managing director calls you in and offers you the job of Mr X's boss Mr Y, who is moving. You ask about Mr X, but the managing director says that you have more ability and potential than Mr X. He says he will have a word with X, but that while he is good at his job, he might not be so good in a more senior position, whereas he thinks you will be. You obviously take the job, but are you feeling delighted or guilty? Both – perhaps you have some worries? What do you say to X after he has seen the managing director.

The answer to that question is quite important. The example is an extreme, but there will be many occasions where you are participating in a situation which is bad news for somebody else. If both yourself and the other person are hardened 'Mr C's', then perhaps there is no problem, but bad news can be hard to handle. Mr X would find it very difficult to avoid making some remarks you might both regret later, and you would find it hard to completely hide your delight at getting the job he wanted.

Mr X was very close to tears as he walked down the corridor and you were the last person he wanted to see. However, he soon gets his feelings under control, at least on the surface. By the following morning just as your elation wears off, he has rationalised the situation – the senior job involved risks, he would be away from home more, the extra money after tax was not worth it, he feels in a better position with you in the hot seat, etc. He has psychologically dried his eyes, and you can meet him without tension.

Sometimes unpleasant decisions are announced in the middle of meetings. Decorum prevents immediate protest from those 'injured' by the decisions, and by the end of the meeting there has been a considerable measure of adjustment to the new situation. The human mind works quickly, but emotions get in the way, and take much more time to adjust.

Summary

To sum up, *the successful manager must work to understand his staff and customers as people*. He must put himself in their shoes and try to appreciate their feelings. Once he has moved towards this understanding he will find them much easier to work with; people respond to those who understand them. People also respond to situations which give them what they want. Self-fulfilment, success and freedom are all subjective matters, and therefore, it is up to the manager to help others to see these as positive parts of their environment.

Change and job satisfaction

The example of the motivated man who had done so much and the frustrated man who has achieved nothing has just been given. The research of American psychologists such as Maslow and Herzberg has suggested that the major factors in motivation at work are contained in the work itself. These factors include achievement, recognition, the actual suitability and congeniality of the work itself and associated matters such as opportunities for responsibility, promotion or acquisition of skills. The demotivators or features which cause frustration and discontent are principally poor (or misunderstood) policies and administration, and bad relationships with one's managers and colleagues.

The question of leadership styles for motivation and results in different situations is discussed in Chapter 3 but this section looks at the psychology of change and how to structure more 'motivation' or satisfaction into work when making changes.

The anatomy in this context of increased job satisfaction breaks down into six rules. The six rules of increased job satisfaction are as follows:

1 Allocate work in natural units or complete transactions.
2 Increase individual responsibility, authority, i.e. job freedom.
3 Reduce routine checks and controls.
4 Issue 'management' control figures and reports direct to those concerned.
5 Introduce new tasks and challenges.
6 Agree specific areas of expertise.

Allocate work in natural units or complete transactions

People feel their work is more important and valid if they handle a complete module, e.g. 'I look after the whole of our business in Yorkshire'; 'I deal with x type of policies from start to finish'; 'I am the link between production control and the rest of the works'; 'I do the whole of the assembly and then pack the widgets for despatch'.

Increase individual responsibility, authority, i.e. job freedom

Wherever possible, let people assume full responsibility for the correctness and quality of their work; let them be responsible for reports or letters produced by them or for clearing work ready for other departments or workstations.

Discretion over pricing rates, refunds, granting of credit, special arrangements, or small differences in sequence and method, etc., can often be granted – to a greater or lesser degree – to responsible junior staff in whom you have confidence. The effect of this type of authority is to broaden the individual concerned and to enable him to demonstrate his potential. Freedom (whether used or not) is a valuable and valued job advantage.

Reduce routine checks and controls

By removing some controls we do not mean reducing accountability. Where mistakes are rectifiable, unlikely or of minor significance, checking can be reduced to sample proportions, but employees who feel they are trusted with something of importance will rise to the responsibility and feel a sense of personal achievement.

Issue management control figures and reports direct to those concerned

Staff are motivated by knowing the results of their work and their achievement against either objective standards, agreed targets, or the requirements of the situation. It is a courtesy and indication of recognition to let them have 'their' results direct and in no way lessens the authority of management and its need to interpret and control.

It is sometimes argued that to pass sophisticated information (e.g. a company's annual report) to junior personnel is a waste of time and paper, but staff (who in some cases are tomorrow's managers) and their families are becoming more widely educated. Given a chance to take a more intelligent interest in the affairs of the organisation, some at least will begin to do so. Even if the figures are not fully understood, the courtesy in distributing them will be appreciated, and the 'we are never told anything' syndrome will be reduced or avoided.

Introduce new tasks and challenges

This is so obvious that it is often overlooked, as most people operate at a far better level of interest and concentration if they are being challenged or stretched (reasonably!) and are having the stimulus of being trained and developed for new tasks. Problems can arise when change is feared or when salary and job grading considerations have been allowed to become barriers to flexibility rather than a system for fair reward.

Agree specific areas of expertise

This rule follows logically from the last. It is not intended that one creates a cadre of indispensable specialists with 'little black books' of exclusive information. What is suggested is that where expertise is required, e.g. legislation, export import formalities, taxation rules, routings, client details etc., that individuals can be given specific areas in which to become conversant. As the individual becomes a subject expert he feels more important and is proud of his 'position'. The subjects themselves become better known in the group and staff know where to turn for help on technical or special matters.

Exercises

1 Describe yourself through the eyes of your main subordinate. Would he or she be irritated, frustrated or disappointed by any of your traits or actions, and what would be seen as your strong points?

2 Describe yourself as seen through the eyes of your boss. Are there any ways in which you could appear to better advantage or be understood more fully?

3 List your subordinates and list against each their main likes or motivations, and their main dislikes or demotivating influences. Do you know them well enough to be reasonably sure you are right?

4 List six main causes of frustration in the department and six causes of job satisfaction (excluding 5 o'clock and payday!).

5 Apply the 'six rules' to the work of your department or office and decide on at least one improvement for each job position.

10 Persuasion and selling

This chapter is very elementary, and it covers rules and precepts which almost everyone reading it will know. Selling and persuading are not very complex activities, but why do we fail so frequently to apply the correct procedures? It must be true that any manager requires a certain minimum of the arts of persuasion for his own use, and sufficient understanding of them to be able to teach and counsel others.

Basic points

If I go to a shop counter and ask for a pound of sausages, the assistant 'sells' me the sausages. He receives my order and processes it to my satisfaction, i.e. to the point where I have paid for the sausages and left the shop with them wrapped up and nestling at the bottom of my shopping basket.

These are very important tasks, but what if the assistant says, 'very good, sir, a pound of sausages – and we have just had delivery of some rather special bacon, see how fresh and moist it is. . .' The assistant is creating a very different situation. He is starting to sell me some bacon, but what he is doing appears not the same as when he sold me the sausages.

However, in both cases the decision is mine, i.e. the buyer. In the first instance I have identified my need for the sausages, whereas in the second it is the assistant who identified my 'need' for the bacon. Of course I may not 'need' the bacon because I do not like bacon, or because I have just bought some elsewhere, or I do not like sharp assistants to push bacon at me, and he has dirty hands and a spotty face anyway, or I may not have enough money to buy the bacon however much I may want it, or I always buy my bacon from the cash and carry, etc. In this case the assistant has 'wasted his time' (and mine), and it is more difficult for him then to say 'and we have some lovely eggs' , than it would be if you had liked the bacon.

Key factors in selling

You may object and say that housewives do not shop like that any longer, but these simple examples illustrate some of the key factors in selling:

1 Selling is creating an opportunity for the buyer to buy.
2 Buyers only buy if they feel they need to.
3 Buyers can only buy if they have the money.
4 Buyers prefer to buy from someone they like and trust.
5 Buyers like to see what they are getting.
6 Buyers like to feel they are getting good value.

Could we rephrase those points and look at them from a managerial aspect? The implementation of change, for example. Change is more acceptable:

1 When it is understood than when it is not. (Explain the reasons, objectives and mechanics of the change.)
2 When it does not seem to threaten security than when it does. (Explain what effects the change will have on the person and his job, the future, and the organisational structure.)
3 When those affected have helped to create it than when it has been externally imposed. (Wherever feasible, develop new methods, procedures, etc., in consultation with those who will be affected.)
4 When it is implemented after prior change has been assimilated than when it is implemented during the adjustment to

other major change. (After each major change, allow for an adjustment period.)

5 When it follows a series of successful changes than when it follows a series of failures. (If several changes over a period of time have failed to solve a problem, it may be better to avoid any further change for a while.)

6 When those affected can see a positive advantage in it. (Explain the benefits of the change, such as better distribution of work-load, more responsibility, better use of talent, more opportunity, training, etc.)

7 When it results from an application of accepted policies or principles than when it is dictated by personal order. (Avoid major change that results only from your personal likes and dislikes.)

8 To people new on a job than to people old on the job. (The more old-timers are affected by the change, the more important it is to apply other principles listed.)

9 When the outcome is reasonably certain. (Where the outcome is uncertain, try the change on an experimental basis for a limited period, for a test area, on a selected number of products. Set up a schedule for follow-up.)

10 If the organisation has been trained to plan for improvement than if the organisation is accustomed to static procedures. (As a manager, encourage suggestions, develop a questioning attitude; establish an understanding that failure of some ideas is considered as part of the cost of progress. Where there is no 'freedom to fail', people will seek the safe, rather than the best solution.)

Final decision

As we saw, buyers or subordinates prefer to buy from someone they like and trust, but no matter how much power a boss may possess, no matter how superior he may be, it is his subordinate who controls the final decision in any change or instruction. It is the employee who ultimately decides to come to work or stay at home; the child decides whether to obey or not. The boss can threaten or persuade, but in the end he is dependent on the subordinate. It is the boss who is motivated, it is he who feels the tension, whose needs are unsatisfied.

The boss represents only one array of forces acting on the employee – he never has complete control. The employee has infinite
techniques for evading, avoiding or retaliating against changes
imposed by his superior.

Criticism

Employees who expect to be criticised whenever they are not working may learn to pretend that they are doing something useful. They
may also learn how far they can take rule-breaking behind
management's back without getting caught. It all becomes a sort of
game.

Frustration and aggression

He knows too that change or conflict may lead to frustration and
hence to aggression or disturbance of some kind. Such a reaction is
normal and the boss should not always take this as a sign of failure or
that he has gone too far. A good idea is to get the subordinate to
take the responsibility for understanding the boss, the situation, the
handling of the change, e.g. getting the student to feel he is responsible for his education rather than the teacher, or at least that the
responsibility is shared. The boss may also be advised to understand
why he acts why he does, what his motives are.

Method of presenting choices

One point which must be stressed, and that is there is a method of
presenting choices, proposals and decisions which is likely to be
more fast and more successful than other ways. Whether it is the
salesman selling bacon, or a director persuading board colleagues,
or a manager talking to his subordinate there is a so-called golden
rule to be observed.

People are not computers; they have logical minds, but they are
also a mixture of feelings, ambitions, frustrations, hopes and fears.
They interpret logical proposals 'logically', but their logic is coloured by these feelings and emotions, whether they know it or not.

The answer is to present every proposal first in terms of the effect
(benefit or advantage) which it will have on the individual himself.
'There is a way in which you can avoid all this searching of the case
papers'; 'this change will enable you to get away on time'; 'this new
car means that you can drive for long distances without strain', etc.

Then follow the benefit by some illustration, visual or physical effect which will stimulate his interest, e.g. charts, photographs, models, drawing on paper, flipcharts, blackboards, mock-up forms, graphs. If possible get him to handle or try it and involve some or all of his physical senses.

Only at the point at which you have identified his interest in the advantages of your point or proposition do you go into such details as are necessary. Remember, too, he may not be so interested in how hard you worked to produce it, where it came from and other data. This may be vital to you, but what is vital to the buyer is what affects him, individually.

Creating the buying situation

I do not advocate 'hard' selling, clever and driving arguments. British people like to buy, not to be pushed into propositions, not to be 'sold'. However, you have to create this buying situation by interesting them in your proposition in the first place and then by listening to them. They will then sell themselves or provide you with clues to objections they have, which you can counter by showing the benefits far outweigh the costs.

Use questions always, e.g. 'how do you feel about that?'; 'what do you think of?'; 'you feel that this is rather expensive . . . what do you think a reasonable price would be for a. . .?'; 'then you feel this might prove useful to you if the price was . . . or if we could deliver by . . . or if you could have it altered to suit . . .'.

However, persuading your man of the advantage of a proposal is not the same as getting him to buy. When you have secured his approval of your proposition always clinch the sale. 'Good, can we get started next Monday?' 'Would next Thursday or Friday be convenient?' 'Would you like to sign the papers now?' 'Can we minute that Mr Smith will present his report to the next meeting?'

Yourself

The motto of one of my schools was *res non verba* – roughly translated as deeds not words (*res* = thing). This is a fine precept, and it would be wonderful to think that our good work, or what would have been good work but for circumstances usually beyond our control or because of the mistakes or omission of others, that our good work should be a sufficient justification and recommendation for ourselves in our working lives. To some extent, and in some occupations, this is so or at least more true than in others, but not in management where we are largely working by controlling and influencing other people. To them we are a voice and an appearance – they see us and hear us. What we look like to them and what we say to them is very literally us.

You will know that each of you appears differently to everyone you come into contact with. People are notoriously subjective about others, and interpret the presentation or outward appearance of those they meet in terms of their emotional history. As for example, if you were bullied at school by a boy with red hair, then men with red hair do not look quite the same to you as they would, for example, to a lady whose first boyfriend had red hair (assuming he did not bully her!). However, you are still left with yourself.

Work measurement teaches us that all work divides down into tiny elements, many repetitive and common to many activities. Psychology teaches us the same is true of our personal mannerisms and speech.

We tend to accept ourselves as we are, but just as we should put ourselves in the shoes of others (empathy) to understand, motivate, influence and help them, we should catalogue our own elements of behaviour and compare them with, as it were, standard practice (see Chapter 4).

How do you speak and look? What sort of people do you get on best with? Think about it – are they the sort of people you are, or were, or think you are, or would like to be? What are their characteristics? Does this analysis tell you anything about yourself?

Where we are dealing with groups, we get on best if somehow we seem part of the group and not as someone different, or a stranger. The exception is if we are cast in some role, e.g. leader, chairman, consultant, doctor, minister, etc., where the group expects us to behave in a particular way. This applies to all encounters with others and we are very much influenced by how people act, appear, and react the first time we meet them.

Meeting other people

A meeting is always a test. A test for both, and it will succeed best if you either seem familiar or have some neutral contact with the other persons. For example compare: 'I was at school with your chairman' with 'my daughter is in the same form as your daughter'.

Comments about mutual acquaintances, places, hobbies and interests, questions which give the other man a chance to talk about his main interest areas, all help. It is also good to be consistent. People pigeonhole you, and if you behave and appear differently to them on different occasions they will react inconsistently too. How do you want to be pigeonholed? If it is as a manager, dress and act like your colleagues would expect a manager to dress and act. Do you?

When talking, prepare or think out what you have in mind beforehand. Do not be rushed into saying something you are not ready to say, or should not say. Many people will try and jump you into saying more than you intend, so work out a number of devices so that you can avoid answering without appearing discourteous in any way, or even interrupting the flow of conversation (see Chapter 9). Examples must relate more to an attitude of mind rather than specific six shooters to draw, but some are given in Chapter 9.

More generally, be interested in what you are saying, without being childishly over-enthusiastic, appear confident and motivated. Look at your opposite numbers, gauge their reactions, pick up their smiles, shrugs, grimaces and other body semantics and show you are with them and understand their feelings (even if you have caused them). If you talk quickly you may lose your hearers and you will fail to emphasise your subject, so talk quickly when you do not want maximum attention, i.e. when talking costs, disadvantages or uninteresting points.

Pauses emphasise the phrases and words immediately before and after them. Speak more slowly and pause to emphasise major benefits and points. Vary your pitch – your audience will soon learn that, for example, you talk a little louder when you need maximum attention from them. Never bore; a monologue in a monotone, with no humour or relief does not endear you to anyone. (But be very careful about actual jokes. I suggest you never use them until you know your audience.)

Listen to your voice on a tape-recorder – see yourself on closed circuit TV playback. See if you have any faults and practise to correct them (see also Chapter 4).

Dealing with senior management

One sometimes sees in job advertisements or descriptions the requirement to be able to negotiate 'at director level'. In the industrial and commercial hierarchy it is sometimes thought and said that 'general' or 'top' or 'senior' management are a different breed of person and behave in a different way from more junior mortals.

From some aspects this must be nonsense, as most top management are promoted junior management; some grooming takes place, but it would seem that senior management are ordinary mortals who are where they are because of experience, special knowledge, ability, and sometimes chance. However, there is an effect which the exercise of power, influence and leadership has on people, and there are certain characteristics which they need to assume. It is an exploration of these features which concerns us now.

A 'boss' never loses his temper. A boss may occasionally be irritable and snappy, but never angry unless he is being deliberately so to achieve some political effect.

You should not lose your temper or self-control with a boss. He may understand, but he will not respect, and as he will never really lose his cool, you lose any status you may have had in the meeting.

Boardrooms are also 'courts'. Men become successful partly because they want the respect and admiration of others. Always they are the target for creepers, none more so than their colleagues who need their co-operation. At board level men are polite and courteous. They are always chatting each other up, always making colleagues and subordinates feel important. You should act politely and directly or indirectly drop whatever compliments you can without being nauseating or fulsome. The compliment must be a clear one, though the better you know the man the more positive and obvious you can become. He will reciprocate and you should be agreeably modest and flattered – on the surface – but underneath you must always be thinking of the next point.

You may wish to disagree with your director or to criticise some aspect of his policy or actions. Of course you should only do this when it might serve some useful purpose, e.g. if there is a disaster which is unlikely to recur, or which was unavoidable it is better to avoid comment. Where there is some chance of your views assisting the director to take a better decision or method of action try and be

tactful. For example: 'with the greatest of respect, sir . . .'; 'you have
obviously taken into account that the union will be opposed. . .'; 'I
did mention, didn't I, that Mr X said he was . . .' Or even a hint
would be enough: 'you did say, sir, you would be seeing Mrs Y first
didn't you . . .'; 'perhaps it's my fault but I didn't quite understand
the bit about . . .'.

Do not be too frightened of your director. Most of them are big
boys and can take quite a few hard knocks. There is a law of nature
which reduces resentment in proportion to the increase in difference in seniority. Equals and near-equals are much more sensitive
than very senior and very junior, though, alas, everyone is too
damned sensitive, about themselves and never about your feelings!

Directors are not always busy men. Good ones control their time
– others may not have many departmental responsibilities, but they
have a wide range of matters in their minds. Their attention span
tends to be very limited, and so if you have 'something to say' make
sure you can say it quickly and succinctly.

'Something to say' is not sufficient. Senior managers are sometimes compared with big guns. They have to be pointed in the right
direction and then fired. Directors accept that many decisions will
have to be made by those below them and accept this role. However, if you point the gun in the wrong direction, then you will cease
to have the directors' trust, and because he cannot or will not spend
the time with you, you are no longer able to get him to use his
position on your behalf.

'Something to say' is something to remember and something to
assimilate when the mind may be full of other things. Some top
managers make lightning decisions, but most sit down and carefully
work through anything important. Therefore, you will find that they
ask you to 'put it in writing'. The ability to put a proposition in
writing is a valuable skill, but it is not part of this chapter. However,
if you have your proposition in writing before you put it verbally,
and when asked to 'put it in writing' you can hand over your piece of
paper there and then, it will have much more impact and can be of a
lower literary standard.

What you propose to the director must be in such a form that he
can assimilate it quickly, and also use it. There are lots of pieces of
interesting information with which you can burden his mind, but
stick to specific proposals he can approve, promote or action. On his
side he may try to put you at your ease with questions about family,

work, etc., but do little more than answer his questions pleasantly and politely. Sometimes he may lead you into talking about matters still under negotiation elsewhere or into making comments on other persons. Do not assume he will respect your confidences, and do not assume that if put in the position of talking to a powerful person of strong personality, when you have not considered in advance what you might say, you may not find yourself saying something ill-considered or which you wished you had not said.

Examples must relate more to an attitude of mind rather than specific six shooters to draw, but compare the following:

MD   –   How is your project getting on?

Self   –   Fine, thanks, the report should be available in three weeks' time.

MD   –   What are you going to propose?

Self   –   Well, we haven't discussed it with the divisional GM yet.

MD   –   But you can tell me – I won't hold you to anything at this stage.

Self   –   . . . . (how do you continue?).

You made your mistake in saying the project was nearly finished. Could 'Fine thanks, we are just discussing the analyses with the DGM' have given him the right lead? But try continuing.

Self   –   Certainly. We are scheduled for a meeting with the DGM next week. Much of our analysis covered the planning in the machine shop as you know and I think you know the problem areas we are dealing with. . . . In fact while I was in the machine shop last week when the buyer from X Ltd., was on his visit and it occurred to me that. . . .

or

Self   –   Certainly. We have been working on a number of alternative solutions to the problem, and I think we can offer you something you will be interested to hear before long. We have a meeting with the DGM scheduled for next week and should be able to present our findings to you shortly after that.

MD   –   Come on, you are holding something back on me, you crafty so and so. . . .

Self   –   Well confidentially, sir, it would help quite consid-
             erably if you could give the DGM some credit for
             the results. Can I fix a meeting for next week? Are
             you likely to be in on Thursday or Friday?

                            or

Self   –   We are not quite ready with the answers yet, but I
             will come and see you or let your secretary know
             just as soon as we have anything ready for you to
             consider. In fact, I would appreciate the opportun-
             ity of discussing this with you again before presen-
             tation as there are going to be some points on
             which I would value your advice or help.

Directors are often involved in political struggles or games. Seldom is there enough power and prestige for all to be satisfied. Big
responsibilities mean big risks and big problems. If you put matters
to them they may want/have to interpret and act on them in the light
of these struggles. They are also accustomed to taking the credit for
work done in their areas. It can gall to see the project you have
slaved on for months suddenly whisked out of your hands and
treated as the work of someone else – and with your name perhaps
never being even mentioned.

There can be cause for concern, but you may find that the great
man recognises your work but is too busy or preoccupied to show it.
Senior managers require results, but they also need them, and are
accustomed to looking for and recognising ability to produce
results. This ability is best displayed by actually producing results.

Agreement by attribution

There is one technique for gaining agreement which has to be used
sometimes – 'agreement by attribution'. This involves attributing an
idea or proposal to someone else – usually the one opposing it, and
can be done by stages, i.e.

Stage 1

Proposer   –   Can we do X?
Senior man –   No.

Stage 2
(Two weeks later, after heavy lunch of senior man)

Proposer   –   You remember you asked me to look into X.
                    Well, I am working on it and I think you were
                    probably quite correct and it will work.
Senior man   –   Confused grunt.

Stage 3
(Two weeks later, similar circumstances)

Proposer   –   I have finished the work on X and you were
                    right after all (eyes shine slightly) . . . . I sup-
                    pose I had better get on and circulate the
                    divisions this week?
Senior man   –   Yes.

This is not a set recipe for success, and the above sequence is a
very crude one to make the point clearly, but it is amazing how often
this type of approach can be introduced into negotiations. Just think
for a moment why it would work, and, of course, we are sure you will
have thought of it yourself already! In fact you mentioned it last
time we met.

A common variant of this game is to attribute the proposal or
support for it to somebody powerful, e.g. the managing director or
chairman; you have to be very sure of your ground if you do this and
you will not be securing acceptance so much as acquiescence, e.g.
'shall I tell the MD then that you don't want to go?', answer 'O.K. all
right, I'll go'.

Phrases to avoid

The following phrases are best avoided:

    as a matter of fact
    so to speak
    you can believe me when I tell you
    it may or may not surprise you to know
    between you and me
    let's put it this way
    more or less
    right
    in other words

in any case
'I'
I think
in my opinion
according to my experience
if I were in your place
I can tell you
take my advice
remember what I said
I must say this
I'm telling you

Avoid also:

Long speeches
confrontation
over- or under-enthusiasm
formality
unfavourable role expectations

Try to achieve:

integration – tune in (shirt-sleeve approach)
working meetings (all 'we' – no 'they')
feedback – a response after not more than 200 words (the response need not always be spoken)

Small language differences

Less good	Better
I think	Don't you think
I can tell you the answer to that	You can work out that answer yourself
You probably haven't thought of that	You're probably aware of
Your certificate must be attached	Please attach your certificate
You didn't conduct that interview very well	Did that interview go as well as you hoped?
Have you any comments to make?	How do you feel about that?
Do this immediately	Can we get started right away?

Selling phrases

Less good

Better

You ought to stock a dozen
of these, we're coming out
with a big ad campaign

You can make a nice profit
from a dozen of these during
our ad campaign

We are buying twice as
much this year, can we have
a price reduction?

Can we think about a bonus
on our yearly turnover?

Suppose you were to die
tomorrow, what would happen
to your family?

Suppose you had died
yesterday, what would have
happened to your family?

How many gallons?

Shall I fill it up?

How many would you like?

Twenty or fifty?

Do you want a salad?

Would you care for a boiled
egg – or a poached egg?

Do you want to buy a tie as
well?

This tie matches your shirt

Anything else (answer 'no')
Is that all (answer 'yes')

When can we meet again to
discuss this?

Would next Tuesday or
Thursday afternoon be
convenient for our next
meeting?
Do you prefer tea or coffee?

Would you like to sign the
order now?

You could sign the authorisa-
tion now, would you like
to use my pen or yours?

Exercises

1   Consider when you last failed to persuade someone else of an
    important point. Analyse the reasons for your lack of success
    and consider how better you could have made your approach.
    What factors would have had most influence on his decision?
2   Which is the most effective in securing acceptance, quality or
    utility?

3   When did you last reject a proposal made to you? What were
     your stated reasons and were they different to your real
     reasons?
4   When did you last accept a proposal made to you? What were
     your motives in accepting, and what did you like in the way the
     proposal was put? Would you have agreed anyway?
5   Are you having difficulties because you cannot persuade some-
     one else to agree with you on a particular matter? (Everyone
     does!) Write down three reasons in the other person's mind for
     disagreeing with you and consider what could be put forward to
     deal with or offset those objections.

Part III

Additional techniques

11 Recruitment: selection and induction

'Yet fish there be, that neither hook nor line,
Nor snare, nor net, nor engine can make thine:
They must be grop'd for, and be tickled too,
Or they will not be catched, whate'er you do.'

John Bunyan

Selection

The purpose of recruitment is, normally, to find the right person for a particular job. The first steps must therefore be to define what the job is, and then what are the likely characteristics of the 'right' person, i.e. a job description and a candidate specification.

This discipline should always be undertaken, as not only does it make the subsequent selection processes easier and more efficient, but it enables the results of the selection (i.e. successes or failures in the job) to be reviewed against the original criteria to see if they need modification. It also helps to offset the bias that every interviewer has for or against particular personal or career characteristics.

Job description

The main headings in a job description will include the following:

1 Job title.

2 Position in company – to whom responsible and details of subordinate positions (if any).
3 Main purpose of job.
4 Key tasks to be carried out.
5 Any special limitations or rules.
6 Characteristics of subsequent work if the position is of a trainee or introductory nature.
7 Location.
8 Conditions of employment.

Candidate specification

The main headings in a candidate specification will include:

1 Age range.
2 Education and qualifications. The possession of a good educational history, and of qualifications indicates a degree of excellence, i.e. intelligence, application, ambition. Qualifications have not been given too much prominence at office level, but it must be borne in mind that with the expansion of further education, the proportion of quick-witted school leavers has dropped. It also means that the proportion of slow-witted persons with further qualifications has increased, and therefore the selection process has to be undertaken with greater care.
3 Experience. This should indicate at least the minimum experience necessary, and the ideal for the job.
4 Personal characteristics. What kind of people get on best with you and your staff. What kind gets on best with the customers, and are there any qualities or characteristics which would help balance your team.
5 Potential/intentions. One should consider the future requirements of the company, and if applicable the division or branch.
6 Background, e.g. mobility, family ties, being 'local', etc.

The first two steps can be considered as 'rules', but the remainder of the selection process is a series of alternative strategies. The manager will have to choose for himself depending on the situation and circumstances, but the subsequent notes offer some suggestions.

Advertising

The ideal advertisement states the company, the job, the location and the salary. However, there are occasions where you have to weaken the impact of the advertisement by using box numbers and vague phrases like 'salary according to experience'. This would be where to be more specific might give away commercially useful information, where you are advertising the job of somebody who is to be replaced or transferred, and where the wages or conditions offered would give rise to jealousy on the part of existing staff. Sometimes you will make a salary offer based on the experience of the successful applicant, but in this case you may really be inviting two or more categories of persons to apply, e.g. intermediate counter clerk or senior counter clerk. You could specify two salary ranges or advertise two jobs.

Remember, *staff are not attracted by vague advertisements*. However, advertising costs money, and as stated above can sometimes be embarrassing. You may have no alternative, but there are two methods you may like to consider:

1 You have a rough general idea of your staff turnover. Keep appropriate contact with the local Employment Service Agency, Professional and Executive Register, etc. Make local contacts and interview likely people on a relaxed basis. Your present or past staff are a good source of contacts once it is known you are ready to chat to interested people. When the vacancy finally occurs, you then have a number of likely candidates to contact.

2 There are not enough experienced staff in, say, the travel trade and, therefore, there is salary competition and 'poaching'. If your budget can stand it there is a lot to be said for taking on a bright school-leaver and bringing him through yourself. As soon as he moves into a more senior position, you bring in another 'trainee'.

Interviewing

Candidates remember interviews. When Company X is mentioned, it is quite common for someone to say 'Oh yes, I was once interviewed by them for a job'. Others may keep quiet for a variety of reasons, but particularly if the interview was a failure. Candidates are not only potential employees, of your company or your competitors, but they are also potential or actual customers, and the effect on them of how the interview is conducted may be significant. For the same reason, correspondence about applications, interviews and results should be prompt and courteous – even if you are only going to indicate a delay.

As soon as I lose interest in a candidate for a job, I am as pleasant as I possibly can be, and try to give the subsequent impression that he or she only just missed a wonderful job with our wonderful firm. It would be unethical to give people too much in the way of false hopes, but it does no good to damage the generally pitifully limited self-confidence of most interviewees.

Interviews take time, and despite your preparation in preparing job descriptions and candidate specifications, and perhaps in applying the techniques described in Chapter 7 you are conscious that you are not a trained job interviewer and that it is a rather occasional exercise as far as you are concerned.

If you can, get applicants to write a letter with personal details, and then get them to fill in an application form. The form ensures that all the personal details are provided for in a standard, and therefore easily compared manner, but it serves another purpose as well. Few applicants keep copies of their original letters, and if they have been 'improving' their particulars you may find discrepancies between the information in the letter and on the form.

It will help if you can send or give the applicant a copy of the job description and any company leaflet or write-up to read before the interview. Likewise you should read his particulars again before he comes in, and in that way the interview is freed from unnecessary discussion. The bulk of the interview should be devoted to an assessment of how he will perform in the job and in the branch.

Interview strategy

The next thing to do is to decide your interview strategy. One should decide whether to have one interview or two interviews. In fact, there is a company which has decided that interviewing is such a faulty process that it selects its 'appointees' on the basis of their applications. I do not suggest that you do this, but it is to be considered whether a single interview will suffice. Interviewees perform differently on different occasions, and so do interviewers, and you may want to see the person twice; you may want somebody else in your office or from another branch or head office to give a second opinion if the results of a wrong choice would be particularly important.

Having decided who is to do the interviewing, how many interviews there are to be, and having done your preparation for them, then the question arises as to how to do the interview. Normally interviews are conducted behind the desk; if you want, however, to be less formal and to get the person being interviewed to be as close and co-operative as possible, then it is better to either sit beside them, or to sit opposite in low chairs to create as 'non-office like' a situation as possible. You may, in fact, decide that you do not want an informal interview; some people advocate that a 'stress' interview is better, because the situation which the person will have to encounter may well be one in which he or she is placed under considerable stress.

A framework or method for the interview should be set up. Where a choice has to be made, and justified, between several candidates, similar questions or tests should be applied. The results and the interviewers' impressions should be noted at the time so as to provide comparative information for the final selection. Obviously, you are comparing each candidate against the job description and candidate specification, and noted up copies of these can be used as an *aide-mémoire* in the interview. Four types of test should be considered:

1 Skill tests.
2 Specific knowledge.
3 Reaction to situations.
4 Intelligence and temperament.

Skill tests
These are tests designed to see how well particular operations can be performed. Examples are asking a typist to type a document, or a clerk to compose a reply to a letter.

Specific knowledge
This would be for persons with some experience. It would involve asking questions about the procedures, products and services relevant to the company, trade or job. Experience and knowledge are related, but there is a difference between the person who can answer 'Yes, I know how to do that. You start by . . .' and the person who can answer 'Yes, I know how to do that and I have done it many

times. You start by. . .'.

Reaction to situations

This is a very valuable test and it offers some of the most reliable pointers to future performance. You describe a situation, perhaps a customer complaint, a refund situation, a cancellation by a supplier or principal, an argument with a colleague, and ask them how they would handle it and what their attitude might be.

Intelligence and temperament

These are scientific tests of various kinds which measure various abilities and aptitudes, and ascertain the weighting of various personality characteristics. As a general rule, tests of this kind should be applied with expert help, but they can provide a specific measure of comparison and a clear indication of ability. It is possible to buy simple intelligence tests which are quite reliable as a measure of mental potential through good booksellers, and to apply them yourself using the directions.

Sometimes, people will be coming to you from a different type of occupation, and a fair test in these cases is to ask them to display their ability in their present job, e.g. if the person has been an assistant in a shoe shop it might be reasonable to ask her to try and sell you a pair of shoes, or if the person has been in an accounts department, it might be an idea to ask her to explain to you the accounts procedure or part of it. While it is difficult perhaps to ask people to display ability in subjects they know nothing about, it is, I think, reasonable to feel that if an applicant cannot perform well in the present job, then one should consider very seriously whether they will perform well in a new job.

Interview length

You have decided your interview strategy, and you must also decide the interview length. It may be that in some cases the interview will run on, but generally speaking the more menial the job, or the more limited the person being interviewed, then the shorter the interview will be. For example, a cleaner's job or an office junior's job may require an interview of 10-20 minutes perhaps, or two interviews of 10 or 20 minutes, if you are going to conduct two interviews, whereas to interview someone for the position of, say, chairman of your company might require several interviews of several hours' duration – not that we are envisaging you being involved in that at the moment!

The choice

Let us skip over the interview now for a little while and consider some other matters which affect the process of interviewing and selection. There is the question as to what to do if two suitable people turn up, or if none at all turn up who are suitable, or if the person who is best as a result of interviews is mediocre, in other words he or she would 'do' but you are not terribly happy. Common sense dictates the answers to these questions with the exception perhaps of the last one.

If an excessively good clerk joins your branch that may present problems; they may be problems which you will probably be happy to have. If you make a real mistake in selection, well then the answer to that situation is also very plain, although with the Employment Protection Act 1975, getting rid of mistakes will become more expensive and more difficult than it used to be. There is, however, a much bigger difficulty in disposing of people who perform reasonably well but not well enough to give you full satisfaction. If one is looking for a rule in a situation like this, the answer is to keep the mediocre person on the hook and keep on looking to try and find somebody in whom you have more confidence.

In an interview you are very dependent on what the candidate tells you. He should, however, have done some preparation, particularly if you have provided him with the job description in advance and company details. It is a good idea to ask him or her whether they know anything about your company. It is a sign of initiative at least if they have taken the trouble to find out something about the work or your office before they come, or at least read what has been sent to them.

I knew a chairman who used to ask applicants whether they thought they could do the job – in others words he shared the decision with the candidate. However, most candidates will press on with an interview whether they think they are suitable or interested or not because they do not like to be rejected. It is quite a boost for the candidate to be offered a job, even if he knows he is going to turn it down; he does not like to think he did not have the chance of turning it down because he was not selected.

One problem which meets the manager is that he may occasionally find somebody who is really suitable – someone he is fully confident in and one he really wants. In such circumstances there may be some merit in offering the job straight away at the interview in order to prevent the candidate from going to other interviews, or at least to discourage him. If a commitment can be obtained there and then you may have forestalled the situation where, when two or three days later the man receives the offer letter, he has already been somewhere else and received another offer.

References

As I said you are very dependent on how the person performs at interview, and this is where references come in. Your company policy may be to have the man checked medically, and to take up written references from previous employers; you may wish to do this anyway, but remember that written references are becoming progressively less useful as a means of identifying people who have some disadvantages, or who have perhaps been unsatisfactory in their previous jobs. (Would you, for example, give a bad reference to somebody who you wanted to get rid of?)

There are also a large number of ways in which written references or references obtained from companies can be falsified. This chapter would be wrong to describe these in writing, but there are a large number of ways in which the 'bent' employee can cover up spells in prison, defalcations, poor recommendations and the like. The least unreliable way of obtaining a reference is to actually telephone the candidate's current manager after the decision to offer the job has been made, and see if, by the way he answers, you can get some reliable information.

Technique of asking questions

You will, of course, be familiar with the technique of asking the same questions more than once at different times in the interview, and note if there is any difference in the answer; also of asking questions obliquely so that the answer to what you really want to know is given off the person's guard. You may also want to ask him questions about things previously discussed to see if he has been concentrating and has learned a point which was made in the exchange.

When the candidate is uncertain

Now, just as you are very dependent on the interviewee's performance at the interview, so he is very dependent on your performance for getting an idea of the job he is to take. In certain cases the candidate will not be certain that the job which you are offering is the one for him or not; this may work two ways, he may take a chance and find subsequently that he wants to leave you, or he may be discouraged and turn the job down, whereas, in fact, he would have been successful and happy with you. If it is at all possible let him meet the other staff, perhaps over a coffee, see where he would be working, get some idea of the work. Careers masters at several schools are now advising young people to do this before taking a job.

Induction

We have considered ways of improving our selection and interviewing, but we can never be completely certain of success. We take a snapshot picture of the applicant and decide on his or her suitability, but the situation is a dynamic one. We have all had the experience where an appointment goes sour on us, and this is not always a mistake in selection although it may appear like one. Many promising recruits are 'ruined' within a few weeks of joining a company, and this section of the chapter sets out some methods of avoiding this.

Basic points

Do you remember your first day at school, your first day at work, your first day in your present job? Days of mixed expectations, hopes, and emotions. Days when impressions and incidents bit deep and went a long way to forming your attitudes to what you had started. Those impressions were important to you, and therefore important to your company – and in particular when you were young, impressionable, and mobile.

Companies go to considerable lengths to attract and employ the 'right' people, but despite the effort and expense many leave after a short period or turn out not to be so 'right' when in the post. Of course mistakes will be made in selection – there are staff for whom the company or work turns out to be not what they thought it would be, or what they wanted, and vice versa – but our experience is that a significant proportion are put off by unsatisfactory happenings in their first days in the job. Their induction procedure has not been planned or implemented in the best way.

Promotions and transfers

Induction also refers to promotions and transfers, and it is most important to ensure that those newly appointed to supervisory positions are given guidance in the practice of managing others so that they get off to the most advantageous start; in this chapter we are concentrating on the first day of the new entrant – a day which may help to mould a man's attitudes to work and to his employer for the rest of his life.

Needs of the company and individual

What does the company want of the new entrant? The company wants:

(a)   him to be doing a useful job quickly;
(b)   to stay and be assimilated;
(c)   to develop as quickly as possible.

On the other hand, the individual wants:

(a)   to respect his employer;
(b)   to understand the purpose of his job and work;
(c)   to be useful;
(d)   to be recognised as a person;
(e)   to see recognition of skills and attainments if he has any;
(f)   to feel 'at home' (social, physiological aspects);
(g)   to enjoy his working life (time at work);
(h)   to see where it is all leading to (next task, career, money prospects, etc.), for him or her.

I would suggest that these needs are very close to each other, unless you take the view that the person just wants to give as little as possible, take as much as he can, or is basically uninterested in anything labelled discipline, respect, learning, work, etc. However, you should consider what you do if he is. Would you act differently?

The important thing is to get him doing a useful and sensible task at the earliest opportunity. Train him for the next task and always give him a little more than you are sure he can handle. Train, stretch, congratulate and make him feel he is moving on as far as he can go. Do not bore good youngsters by keeping them on routine or 'junior' jobs too long.

Day of arrival

See the new entrant when he arrives, and give him a 10–20 minute chat before you settle him down to his first task. That talk is a situation of some tension for both sides, and should be prepared and adjusted to the circumstances. We suggest you do not overwhelm him with all the background all at once – remember he is just as concerned with minor administration matters, e.g. where to put his coat, position of toilets, lunch, coffee, etc., in the first day or two.

However, he should be told the following:

1 The general scale and organisation of the company.
2 What types of business are transacted.
3 Any special features about the branch.
4 The purpose of what he does, and why he was recruited.
5 What he will do next. (These are questions which his relatives and friends will ask him on his return.)
6 Your position, authority. Local and company rules and etiquette. (You are the company to him. If you are cheerful, enthusiastic, competent, what will he think? On the other hand, if you are cynical, hardbitten, short, over-busy what does he then think? Who does he see in you? Himself in 10–20 years?)

Answer his questions, but do not spend too long chatting. He came to work and wants to be useful. Get him doing something useful. Get him doing something useful and relevant without delay.

Only one rule: do not overdo trying to elaborate an induction but do spend time with him at the beginning, and do not ignore him for any long period as you are very important to him.

Some organisations have printed induction booklets but it can be a good idea to give him a little outline plan of the office with colleagues names, your own name and title, telephone number and other important points he might easily forget to his embarrassment in the first day or so.

Come back to him at intervals. Encourage him, give him more tasks, more training. Do not let him get away with anything sloppy, but be patient until he has got the message.

Induction checklist

The following checklist summarises the main points to bear in mind, although of course each individual will need to be treated on his or her own merits. However, if you are too busy to see your new staff member when he joins, just consider what will be going on in his mind.

Tell the new entrant the following points:

1 Who and what you are. How he should address you.
2 The job, section and branch titles.
3 Check what his experience and skill is, if any, and any proclivities he may have.
4 Work times, coffee, lunch, tea, cloakroom arrangements, his desk, stationery, how and when pay comes and any rules.
5 The company, i.e. its business and the business of the branch or department.
6 His colleagues – introduce them and hand out or construct with him a list of their names and functions and any points of style which may help him.
7 Any questions – answer them.

People learn fastest and work best for supervision they respect and like. Does your induction procedure, appearance and style command respect, or does it need to be more helpful, polite, efficient, enthusiastic, disciplined, etc? Perhaps if he is not learning then you are not teaching him the right way. Remember that 'there are no bad staff, only bad supervisors and managers'.

Exercises

1 Prepare a job description for your own job and have it discussed and agreed by your superiors.
2 Prepare a job specification for your job and compare it with your own particulars.
3 Prepare and agree job descriptions for your subordinates, and in particular a deputy. Whether you have one or not.
4 Prepare a ten-minute induction talk (about 1,500 words, but it

could be done in headings) and use it when the next recruit arrives in your department.

12 Appraisal and counselling

'A soft answer turneth away wrath: but grievous words stir up anger.'

Proverbs XV

Appraisal

We are appraising each other, consciously and subconsciously most of the time; our subordinates judge us, and we judge them. Everybody is forming views, or confirming previous impressions of others all the time. It gives us a natural satisfaction to understand how people react and feel.

Likewise we are happy to advise or counsel others whenever they ask us or when we feel the conditions are right – providing always that the situation is such in which our advice or comment is not going to cause resentment. We like to help others, and to a considerable extent appraisal and counselling are about helping others. How?

Appraisal and counselling become 'subjects' because in the pressure of normal business we may not spend enough time or give sufficient consideration to them. We have to make sure they are done in a structural fashion, and that we prepare ourselves to give proper attention to all the necessary aspects. Information has to be sought and given. Proper communication must be established.

Matters to be established

Various matters need to be established, though not necessarily all at the same time. These will include:

1 Review of performance and achievements.
2 Points of weakness and warnings.
3 Training and development needs.
4 Fitness in work, job satisfaction.
5 Prospects, career development.
6 Review of job description and requirements.
7 Salary review.
8 Manpower planning assessments ('tiering').
9 Personal matters.

You may not have the answers for everything, and there is a limit to magic wand waving in any situation. However, the interviewee expects positive suggestions, actions and follow-up, and the good manager prepares in advance by thinking of what could and might be done.

Criticism

Criticism, we said, raises defensive issues, leads to arguments, and has a negative effect on subsequent performance. However, we cannot avoid some criticism, even if it is done by implication, and there are occasions when the errors are of such a significance that they have to be dealt with explicitly and formally. This is a problem, and the reason is simply that the other person feels he is being attacked. The fact that the attack is psychological not physical, makes it none the less real, but more difficult to control.

Praise

We put forward a case for participation and objectivity, but there are two other lines to consider. One is praise. Every employee will have done, or intended to do, something useful (otherwise he should not be on your staff!) and this should be recognised straight away at the start of any review session. Salesmen call this the sandwich technique, i.e. starting and finishing a discussion with something which is attractive, or appealing to the other's ego – 'sugaring the pill'. Praise or recognition must be part of the review, but it can be used to balance the bad news. 'You have made a good start on such and such, and now you can really begin to tie things together by. . . .'

Constructive suggestions

The other point is to put forward constructive suggestions. Criticism is discouraging, but positive proposals for new standards, goals or objectives, or for training, advice or help have an encouraging effect. This is particularly so where the employee has suggested or contributed to the proposals. There must be a clear method or means of obtaining the required improvement – the employee must feel he knows (and approves) what is required, and how he can produce it. These points will be considered in more detail, but they represent a formidable list.

Appraisal sessions

Many managers view a cold-blooded appraisal session with apprehension, and rightly so. Such interviews are very sensitive and personal and can easily lead to misunderstandings. They invite proposals for action on either side, which may in themselves create problems or be difficult to follow-up. Some pointers can be listed.

Criticism may result in elimination of faults e.g. 'All right, you want it that way, you'll get it that way', but it has a negative effect on subsequent motivation. However well intentioned, it leads to a defensive attitude on the part of the person being assessed, and even if he recognises the fault, he may feel your method of presenting it is unfair. (What does he know about it anyway?)

The American behavioural scientist Rensis Likert suggests an approach – 'People seem most willing and emotionally able to accept, and to examine in a non-defensive manner, information about themselves and their behaviour, including their inadequacies when it is in the form of objective evidence'. State the case, if you have to, but try not to say 'I feel you are. . . . I think you are. . . . etc.' Try rather – 'These are your results for the last month, showing actual against target figures. How do you feel about the situation?' or 'Is . . . going as well as you'd hoped?' Even a simple 'is there anything I can do to help?' may encourage the interviewee to start discussing his own perceived shortcomings with you, and you are then beginning to see the openings you need. If a man criticises himself he feels he is participating, he is directing attention to areas which he wants discussing, he feels the interview, qua Likert, is 'objective'.

To sum up, there are four keynotes to strike in the successful review:

1 Praise for achievement and intentions.
2 Participation at all points.
3 Objective approach to problems.
4 Means of obtaining specific improvements.

We have looked at the climate and approach to the assessment. Each company will be using the assessment procedure for slightly different purposes, dependent on their policies, and obviously whoever is doing the assessments must know what those purposes are. For completeness and standardisation assessments are written on a form; your company may have one already. Three examples are given at the end of this chapter (Figs. 12.1–12.3).

Most of assessment is common sense, but we list now the steps involved in the concept, or in preparation.

The six principles

1 What are we trying to appraise? Competence in job and value to company.
2 What criteria or qualities would be used to judge competence? Go for criteria which are concrete and measurable. Go for the ones which really give a measure of performance. Output. Quality. Job knowledge, product knowledge, customer relations, co-operation, initiative, discipline and bearing. Let us decide how many criteria we will use and rank them in order of importance.
3 What framework will we use? Refer to the specimen forms. Consider what descriptions would be best. Unsatisfactory, satisfactory, very good, outstanding, unproved. Does not meet requirements, needs some improvement, meets job requirements, exceeds requirements, far exceeds requirements, etc. Five is the normal range of rankings.
4 How often will we appraise? Consider salary and cost of living

reviews. Every six months is considered good practice for formal appraisals.

5 Who should do it? The manager should know the person best, therefore he can assess performance comprehensively and objectively; he can identify and offer assistance where performance is below par and give praise and recognition where it is above par. Is anyone else involved? Who, if anyone, should receive copies of the assessments? Should there be second opinions or appeals? Apart from the manager and the employee, can anyone take action to help?

6 How much should staff be told? Should the interviewee see all or part of the final assessment, and should the form be completed in conjunction with him? The employee wants to know how he is regarded on one hand, but on the other the assessor or manager may find it embarrassing to be completely frank, and to show critical comments in writing. Some companies have a two part assessment, in which the employee sees and signs one part, but there is a confidential section which is not seen. This chapter does not offer an answer to this question; the management style of the company may provide an answer, but it is axiomatic that nothing should be done which does not strengthen the relationship between the management and employees or which damages any person's self-confidence. If you cannot be frank with your employees what does that tell you about your own management style. Will the staff think you are being 'honest' with them?

Counselling

Part of an assessment review is advice and determination of action to obtain improvements, i.e. counselling is involved. However, there are specific counselling interviews, initiated by the member of staff or by his manager, to deal with particular problems, often of a personal nature.

The manager may be in a good position to help with private problems, and it may be appropriate for him to do so, either in his managerial capacity or just as any human being will try to help another. He is, however, employed primarily to keep the business going, and he is a manager and not a psychiatrist.

STRICTLY PRIVATE AND CONFIDENTIAL

STAFF PERFORMANCE REPORT

SURNAME .... FIRST NAME(S) ....

Date of birth ....

DEPARTMENT .... JOB TITLE .... GRADE ....

Length of Service in .... Length of time in present job ....

Date of Previous Review ....

PART 1 To be completed by Job Holder

  i. Have there been any special office or domestic circumstances that have affected your performance of the job during the period under review?

    Please answer Yes or No .... If "Yes", what were they?

  ii. Are there ways in which the Company can help you do your job better?

  iii. Would you like the opportunity to change your job within the Company?

    Please answer Yes or No ....

    If "Yes", please explain what jobs you would prefer and why? Are there any abilities which you possess that you feel can be useful to the Company in other work? For example, previous business experience, further education or personal aptitudes.

Date ....   Signed ....

Fig. 12.1 Specimen staff performance report

PART 2   To be completed by the Job Holder's immediate superior

From the assessment on the Merit Rating form PART 3 and your
knowledge of the staff member please indicate:

 i. What are the member of staff's strong points?

 ii. What points need improving?

 iii. How are you helping the Job Holder to improve on these points?

 iv. How do you intend to develop this member of staff during the next
      review period?

 v. Overall Assessment from PART 3.

 vi. Previous overall assessment.

 vii. General comments which should include any aspects of the Job Holder's
       qualities or performance that are not covered above.

Fig. 12.1 (continued)

PART 3. MERIT RATING ASSESSMENT.   SURNAME & INITIALS ....   DATE ....

FACTOR	DOES NOT YET MEET REQUIREMENTS (1)	NEEDS SOME IMPROVEMENTS (2)	MEETS JOB REQUIREMENTS (3)	EXCEEDS JOB REQUIREMENTS (4)	FAR EXCEEDS JOB REQUIREMENTS (5)
A. Output (Compared with standard)	Slow	Reasonable but not yet up to standard.	Satisfactory Output to standard.	Works hard. Gets through more work than most.	Exceptionally quick and industrious worker.
B. Quality/accuracy. (Compared with standard)	Inclined to make mistakes. Needs checking/close supervision.	Makes only few mistakes. Work reasonable.	Reliable and accurate. Very few mistakes. Satisfactory.	Good worker. Completely reliable and accurate.	Unusually good.
C. Job knowledge.	New to the work. Needs help or direction to cope with the normal aspects of work.	Copes with all the regular aspects of the work with only routine supervision.	Able to perform the work virtually in all aspects. Occasional direction needed.	Complete knowledge of work. Can impart knowledge to others. Better than most.	Outstandingly capable, sound and complete knowledge of work. Very experienced.
D. Co-operation.	Co-operates reluctantly.	Co-operative. Reasonably receptive to instructions.	Co-operative and accepts instructions willingly.	Very co-operative and flexible.	Exceptionally helpful.
E. Initiative.	Shows no initiative.	Sometimes misses opportunities to show initiative.	Shows initiative required of the job.	Has particularly sound and practical ideas.	Extremely flexible and quick on the uptake. An example to the department.
F. Discipline/bearing.	Not a good timekeeper. Inclined to waste time. Presentation needs to be improved. Requires warning.	Satisfactory.	Good. Conscientious employee.	A good example and very conscientious.	Extremely conscientious in every way. Bearing and conduct exemplary.

Overall assessment : Taking all factors into consideration, tick the phrase which most accurately describes the employee relative to your standard of a satisfactory performance of the work and complete PART 2 Q.V.

1. *DOES NOT YET MEET REQUIREMENTS.*
   Only acceptable for a starter, below standard and must improve to be retained in existing job.
2. *NEEDS SOME IMPROVEMENT.*
   Regarded as adequate.
3. *MEETS JOB REQUIREMENTS.*
   A good employee.

4. *EXCEEDS JOB REQUIREMENTS.*
   A very good employee, ready to be considered for promotion.
5. *FAR EXCEEDS JOB REQUIREMENTS.*
   A very good employee in all respects
   (a) does not seek promotion
   or (b) promotion is overdue.

Fig. 12.1 (continued)

FACTOR	BELOW STANDARD (1)	ROOM FOR IMPROVEMENT (2)	EXPERIENCED (3)	ABOVE AVERAGE (4)	SUPERIOR (5)
1. *Job knowledge* How is he/she coping with the work. Has he/she learnt the work. Is help needed.	New to the work. Needing help or direction to cope with the normal aspects of work.	Coping with all the regular aspects of the work with only routine supervision.	Able to perform the work virtually in all aspects. Occasional direction needed.	Complete knowledge of work. Can impart knowledge to others. Better than most.	Outstandingly capable, sound and complete knowledge of work. Very experienced.
2. *Productivity* Output of work compared with standard (not quality or accuracy).	Slow	Reasonable but not satisfactory.	Satisfactory. Output to standard.	Works hard. Gets through more work than most.	Exceptionally quick and industrious worker.
3. *Quality* Is the work performed in a reliable and accurate manner.	Inclined to forget and make mistakes. Needs checking/close supervision.	Makes only few mistakes. Work reasonable.	Reliable and accurate. Very few mistakes. Satisfactory.	Good worker. Completely reliable and accurate.	Unusually good.
4. *Co-operation/initiative* Is he/she co-operative, willing to help others, to organize his/her work.	Co-operates reluctantly. Can be a source of friction.	Co-operative. Reasonably receptive to instructions.	Co-operative and accepts instructions willingly. Organises work well. Fits in well and is flexible.	Very co-operative and has sound and practical ideas. Sensible and flexible.	Exceptionally helpful and constructive, flexible and quick on the uptake. An example to the department.
5. *Discipline/bearing* Does he/she start work promptly and continue until time to stop. Is his/her presentation reasonable.	Not a good timekeeper. Inclined to waste time. Presentation needs to be improved. Often requires warning.	Satisfactory.	Good. Conscientious employee.	A good example and very conscientious.	Extremely conscientious in every way. Bearing and conduct exemplary.

Overall assessment: Taking all factors into consideration, tick the phrase which most accurately describes the employee relative to your standard of a satisfactory performance of the work.

1. Only acceptable for a starter, below standard and must improve to be retained. ....
2. Regarded as adequate.
3. A good employee.

4. A very good employee, ready to be considered for promotion. ....
5. A very good employee is all respects but doesn't seek promotion or promotion is overdue. ....

Fig. 12.2 Merit rating guide

Part One. In this part you should appraise the employee's strengths and weaknesses as shown by performance during the year. Mark each separate quality out of six (marks will not be totalled).

Very good indeed	6	Some problems	3
Quite satisfactory	5	Not satisfactory	2
Average	4	Untrained or untried	1

A). Performance in work.	Marks.
Knowledge and experience Application Adaptability Accuracy Supervisory ability. General assessment.	
B). Mental ability.	
C). Relations with others.	
D). Maturity and judgement.	

Part Two. In this part you should make specific comments under the following headings:

Job successes and job failures.

Particular strengths and weaknesses.

Training and courses attended during past year – planned further training

Development potential, future plans for promotion or transfer.

Morale and attitude to work and company.

Additional remarks, including employee's points at assessment interview.

NAME.............................. ......   DATE.............   ASSESSOR.....................

Fig. 12.3 Specimen assessment form

Each manager must use his own judgement, but he should be careful about getting involved in difficult personal problems which he may not be able to handle. In such cases the company personnel manager should be contacted, and if this is not feasible there are many points of help locally, e.g. social services departments, family planning associations, marriage guidance councils, citizens advice bureaux, the Samaritans, your, or his, lawyer, doctor, bank manager, minister, etc.

Staff should always feel they can approach you, and that you 'care', even if you do not provide all the answers yourself personally.

Exercises

1   Decide whether you want or need to install a formal appraisal and counselling system.
2   Consider whether there is any policy or experience in appraisals elsewhere in the organisation you should consult, and whether you should develop a system in co-operation or on your own.
3   Define your attitude to the six principles on p.126.
4   Design your own appraisal form or checklist.

13 Teaching and learning

'If the worker hasn't learned, then the trainer hasn't taught.'

Most managers can and do train subordinates and colleagues, and the world is full of people struggling to remember what to do, or putting mistakes right. This chapter sets out a method for training quickly and effectively, and it may help you save time both of yourself and your staff when next you become involved in the process.

Method

Concentration is difficult, so avoid anything which causes distractions or tensions. Has the trainee made himself comfortable and have you left instructions about phone calls and interruptions? Put him at ease – instruction is better at his desk or work position, or in neutral surroundings. It is better to sit beside him than talk with a desk between you.

Now start by telling him exactly what you are trying to do, e.g. 'I would like us to spend half an hour this afternoon checking through the requisitioning procedure' or, 'would you like us to start looking at the XYZ machine so that you can begin to learn how to use it?'

Then, find out what he knows, or thinks he knows about it already. Unbeknown to you, he may have had some experience or discussion on the subject elsewhere which may be relevant.

Next, tell him, if you have not already said, why he should learn what you are teaching. 'This is the way we obtain the stationery, pencils, rubbers or similar things we use in the office. I would like you to learn this, so that you can take it over from Mary', or 'we use this machine to cut the threads on the special bolts which support the girders in the crane assembly', or 'it is worth getting to know how to use this procedure so that when Joe or myself are away, you will be able to deal with any service requests'. Get his interest – make sure he sees some point in learning the job – and show your own appreciation of the importance or interest of the task.

Demonstration

At this point you can explain the job or procedure. If any forms or equipment are involved, have them there to show wherever possible, and explain any technical terms, jargon or abbreviations. Demonstration, 'show-how', is invaluable, and if you can, run over the job quietly at this stage so that the trainee can learn by watching and get an overall view of the procedure.

Now think how much you are likely to be able to teach him on this occasion. Persons whose minds have not been trained beyond 'O' level cannot concentrate in general for more than about 10 minutes on a 'lecture'. Break up what you say to them into natural units, preferably 150-200 words, or one to two minutes depending on how fast you talk, and let them react or catch up, e.g. 'Are you with me so far?' They can concentrate on 'doing' better than listening, but it is far better to teach a little but thoroughly, rather than confuse by covering too much ground.

Professional staff or graduates can concentrate for longer periods, say up to forty minutes, though it may be more difficult to hold their interest. Older people find it harder to learn new subjects, though they will often appear to follow what you say when they do not want to seem stupid.

So demonstrate the job again, in key stages one at a time, and explaining fully in detail each stage as you go. Answer questions with tolerance and patience – everyone has a blank period from time to time. Do not go on beyond the point at which confusion sets in. 'Well, that's about far enough for just now, let's have a recap, and then you can try it out.'

Trying out

Next get him to try out what you have just taught him, in stages, and with you watching. Do not let him run ahead, because it is just as easy to do the wrong thing as the right, and then the wrong thing has to be unlearned before he can get it right. Do not let him run through because he may do the right things by mistake.

Point out any errors as they arise; be helpful, not critical. If he makes a real mess, ask him for his own opinion. 'How do you feel about that particular result?' 'How do you think that went?' 'What happened that time?' 'What went wrong?' Try not to damage his confidence, 'Well done, you are getting the idea, but it still isn't quite there. Shall we have another go, and this time concentrate more on getting the discount calculations exact!'

Questions

In due course ask him questions about the job and each stage of it to make sure he really understands what he is doing. Use your critical analysis questions, e.g. How do you do that? Why is that done? Where is that done, where does that go? When does that happen? What does that achieve? Who does that part of it, which departments are involved?

Carry on until you are sure he knows the job and, of course, that he has the necessary confidence that comes from proper training.

At that point he can start on his own – 'the deep end' – but never throw him in just like that. Make sure he knows who to turn to if he forgets something or if an unexpected situation arises. Do not ignore him – show that you are still interested in the job and his performance by checking with him, often at first, less often as he becomes proficient. See if he has any questions and comments – people often like to make a comment to share their experience: 'it makes your hands tingle doesn't it', 'hot work today', 'don't know how I got away with that one', etc.

Do please ask one question if you have not already done so. Would not a manager who instructs like this get right up the nose of his staff? Phrases like 'insulting my intelligence' or 'fussy beggar' come to mind. 'Treat us like adults' they cry, and then proceed to get it wrong. The steps in this chapter can be very helpful, but only if you have a good working understanding with your subordinates.

By now the trainee should have settled down to the job under normal supervision. You have done a solid piece of training and you can tick off another task achieved on your training plan. You can trust him, and he feels you should. But alas, managers are not paid to ignore their staff. You must continue to show interest and you must from time to time sit down with him and just see what he is actually doing. Is it in accordance with the procedure, is it right? You can only do this without offence or unease if you have that same relationship with your staff that comes through regular contact. What is regular contact? I leave that to you, but once a day used to be my rule. You also get that vital ingredient in control and communications – feedback.

Exercises

Ask yourself a few questions.

1   When did you last learn a major new task or procedure?
2   Were you taught, did you teach yourself? Did you learn it satisfactorily, or could it have been handled better?
3   Are internal memos or instructions sufficient for most staff to absorb changes?
4   How should training manuals be set out?
5   Have you a training plan? (See Chapter 6.)
6   How are your staff trained? Should you be involved more or less? If they are trained by others, are you satisfied with their training technique?
7   Are there any courses which would help? How could you justify them?
8   What is the difference in cost to the organisation of a person being taught on a two week course and starting the job as 80 per cent proficient, and the same clerk taking ten weeks to become 80 per cent proficient (assuming a straight learning

'curve' from zero to 80 per cent during the period) by learning 'on the job'?

Cost of course – £240.

Cost of person – £100 per week.

Answer – 'value' in first case.

8 weeks × 80% of £100 = £640 – £240 cost of course = £400.

in second case

10 weeks × 40% of £100 = £400.

9 Would you rather have properly trained people in your department, or have them milling around trying to pick up the job, and perhaps making expensive mistakes?

10 Is the value of staff their wages or is there another value?

14 The assessment and improvement of work

'A practical man is a man who practises the errors of his fore-fathers.'

Disraeli

Introduction

In Chapter 2 a method was put forward for using diary sheets and work distribution charts to enable the manager to get an overall view of how he was spending his own time, prior to constructive analysis of his activities. The same approach can be applied to the work in your department as a whole, and this chapter indicates how this can be done. The result will be that you will finish up with information as to how long each of the activities in your area takes, or alternatively an estimated work content for each transaction.

It need hardly be pointed out what the value of this kind of information is in costing and planning, and in the improvement of procedures. Subsequent chapters will explain in more detail how these can be progressed from the basic information obtained through the method. (Of course, if you have already got detailed measurement in your area, then you should not need to read this chapter.)

To examine the work in your department in proper perspective you need a picture of the area as a whole plus individual breakdowns of the work of each individual.

Activity list

The activity list should be prepared by yourself, and should include all of the major activities that are performed, or that should be performed to fulfil the objectives of the department. Thus if, for example, a personnel manager felt that wage and salary surveys was an activity which his department should perform but was not doing at the present, it should go on the list. This would show, of course, that you were aware of a need but were unable to devote any time at the present juncture. A 'miscellaneous' heading is usually required for the odd jobs that do not contribute directly to the real purpose of the department. An example of the heading of an activity list is shown in Fig. 14.1.

Task list

The task list is a detailed record of each separate item of work performed by the individual. Each employee, including of course yourself, prepares his own list to ensure a clear coherent story, and you will later review these lists with your subordinates. Obviously the lists must be as complete as possible and the wording should be specific and not ambiguous; by ambiguous I mean expressions such as 'checking' and 'administration'. The type of entries that should appear on the task list might be, for example, 'checking arrival of incoming shipments', 'checking invoices against purchase orders and goods received notes', 'replenishing stationery cupboards', 'drawing stores' etc. An example of the heading of a task list is shown in Fig. 14.2.

Time taken for each activity

You will see in the task list that provision is put in for the time taken for each activity. It may be that a common sense answer in terms of representative times or estimates can be produced from estimates or records, but more usually it is obtained by asking the person or persons concerned to keep a simple record for a few days.

DEPARTMENT:	SECTION:	SUPERVISOR:	DATE:
ACTIVITY NO.	ACTIVITY (FUNCTIONS)		

Fig. 14.1 Activity list for work distribution chart

Idle time

In most functions there will be idle time, time for resting and delays, time awaiting work and other non-productive time in every day's work. Even in the most well organised situation, about one-sixth of the available hours is lost on average through chatting, smoking,

NAME:		OCCUPATION or TITLE:	CLASSIFICATION:		
DEPARTMENT:	SECTION:	SUPERVISOR:	DATE:		
TASK NUMBER	DESCRIPTION		QUANTITY	POSTED TO ACTIVITY NO.	HOURS PER WEEK
			TOTAL		

Fig. 14.2 Task list for work distribution chart

personal needs, and all the other incidentals like dropping pencils on the floor, hanging up one's coat, having a drink of tea, etc. However, there are going to be a great many occasions when the majority of the staff, and doubtless the manager as well, has no clear idea how long different tasks take. This is particularly the case in office situations where tasks are often interrupted and in some cases several jobs are performed or attempted at once. In these cases a diary sheet or a tally form is usually the answer.

Diary sheet

The diary sheet is used in conjunction with the task list; you will see from the specimen diary sheets that all that is done is that as one moves from one task to another, one puts the number of the ensuing task against the quarter hour slot in which it was started. Interruptions and telephone calls are entered by tally marks, just as in the case of your own task list. The diary sheets are run for a common sense period of time. In a department which performs much the same work from one week to the next, a fortnight may well be sufficient to give a representative breakdown of the work. In other areas, for example in an accounts department, the cycle might be monthly and, therefore, the diary sheets will need to be run for a month. There are occasionally areas where the cycle is of much longer duration than one month, but in these cases one day per week on a staggered basis over the appropriate period, for example, would provide a reasonable answer. Examples of diary sheets are given in Figs. 14.3 and 14.4.

Reason for diary sheets

It is quite usual for staff to make a mess of the first day or two days' diary sheets through unfamiliarity, however well you explain the situation. I would normally throw away the first two days and then use the subsequent ones for the analysis. One must, of course, explain fully to the employees why the diary sheets are being produced; employees should be told that they are not being timed personally or being asked to account for every minute of their day for future use in controlling them more tightly. When employees have a chance to demonstrate what they do, to demonstrate the complexity of their work, and to contribute to a study that might lead to better planning or more equitable distribution of work, they are normally only too pleased.

When the diary sheets have been completed you should first review the activity list and see whether the original analysis you made still stands. You should then transfer the activities, in the order of their importance, to the column provided in the work distribution chart.

Work distribution chart

An example of a work distribution chart is shown in Fig. 14.5.

You should review the task lists with the individual employees, and then set them in order of their importance, with your own list, if appropriate, on top. Then put your subordinates' names and other pertinent data on top of the work distribution chart, starting with yourself in the first column, if relevant, and then work from left to right. Of course, if additional columns are required an extra sheet may be pasted on.

Now review each item on the task lists and enter the corresponding activity number, then transfer the separate tasks and hours to the space provided opposite the appropriate activity on the work distribution chart. You may, of course, combine two or more separate tasks listed by a subordinate into one task, but make sure this task, with its activity number, is noted on the employee copy. If you are going to alter the hours shown on the task lists and diary sheets, it would be as well to discuss this with the subordinate concerned.

Clear and full picture available

After all the hours and tasks have been recorded, add up the total hours both vertically and horizontally to show totals for each subordinate, the entire department, and each activity. Your chart now gives you a clear and full picture of your department and its work.

The information you have in front of you now on the work distribution chart is not completely accurate, nor is it work measurement in any classical sense of the term. What you have got is a reasonably accurate and common sense picture of the proportions of time of the department as a whole and of the individuals involved which are spent on the different activities. This information can be used for three main purposes, for improvement, for cost evaluation, and for planning and control.

Improvement

Let us take first the question of improvement. Anyone can have a

Time	Item No.	Interruptions Phone	Interruptions Other	Quantities	Item No.	Description	Total Time	Total Unit	Unit Time
8.00						(as task list)			
.15									
.30									
.45									
9.00									
.15									
.30									
.45									
10.00									
.15									
.30									
.45									
11.00									
.15									
.30									
.45									
12.00									
.15									
.30									
.45									
1.00									
.15									
.30									
.45									
2.00									
.15									
.30									
.45									
3.00									
.15									
.30									
.45									
4.00						(Detail telephone and other interruptions here)			
.15									
.30									
.45									
5.00									
.15									
.30									
.45									
6.00									

Title .... Name ....
Date .... Dept. ....

Fig. 14.3 Diary sheet

Department:			Name:		Title:	Date:
Time	Item No.	Quantity	\multicolumn{4}{c}{INTERRUPTIONS}
			Phone	Other	\multicolumn{2}{c}{Details}
8.15						
.30						
.45						
9.00						
.15						
.30						
.45						
10.00						
.15						
.30						
.45						
11.00						
.15						
.30						
.45						
12.00						
.15						
.30						
.45						
1.00						
.15						
.30						
.45						
2.00						
.15						
.30						
.45						
3.00						
.15						
.30						
.45						
4.00						
.15						
.30						
.45						
5.00						
.15						
.30						
.45						
6.00						

Fig. 14.4 Daily diary sheets (another example)

ORGANISATIONAL UNIT CHARTED: .... Cha. by .... Apprd. by .... Chart Date .... ☐ PRESENT ☐ PROPOSED Covering ☐ Weeks diaries				(1) Name & (2) Position 1 2	1 2	1 2	1 2	1 2	1 2	1 2	1 2	1 2	1 2	1 2	1 2	1 2	1 2	1 2	1 2	1 2	1 2	1 2	1 2	1 2
NO.	ACTIVITIES (Functions) & TASKS (Jobs)	Quantities	TOT. HRS.	HRS.	HRS.	HRS.	HRS.	HRS.	HRS.	HRS.	HRS.	HRS.	HRS.	HRS.	HRS.	HRS.	HRS.	HRS.	HRS.	HRS.	HRS.	HRS.	HRS.	HRS.
	(Enter first activity, then all tasks related to that activity, then proceed to the next activity).																							
	INSERT SUB-TOTALS OR TOTALS (MANHOURS)																							

Fig. 14.5 Work distribution chart

flash of inspiration, but most improvements in industrial and commercial organisations are obtained through the use of disciplined approach to any data provided. One of these approaches is called critical analysis, and in this we ask ourselves six questions about each major point in any data which is the subject of our investigation. The questions are why? what? where? when? who? and how?

Why and what?

Having prepared our work distribution chart we can ask first two questions, 'why' and 'what'. We ask ourselves 'why is this activity necessary?' Is it properly a function? and then we say 'what does this activity accomplish?' Is it cost effective, or is the amount of time shown a reasonable amount of time for this activity as a percentage of the whole? We are going to go over each activity to see if it makes sense to perform it at all, see whether it is absolutely necessary or whether it is duplicated by another department. We are going to see whether the activities are in keeping with the objectives of the department and, incidentally, whether the objectives of our department are in keeping with the needs of the company.

The second stage is to read horizontally across the chart and look at one task at a time. For this step we will use the questions 'where', 'when', 'who' and 'how'.

Where?

Where in the department or in the company should this task be done? Consider available skills, equipment, files, similar reports, the layout, where similar work is done. Obviously one either wants to transfer the activity to the area where you have least overall cost, or if cost is not so important, where it will be conducted most efficiently.

When?

In what part of the day or of the week, or of the month, should this task be performed? Does it need rescheduling to balance the daily workload, or should it be batched to save a lot of preparation and putting away elements? When, in fact, is it required? Is it required hourly, daily, weekly or monthly, or have we checked recently to find out whether if our present deadlines coincide with the real requirements, or whether for example, half of the data would be sufficient to get the next department started? Would an estimate, projection, or rounded figures do just as well?

Who?

Who does this? Who has the skill needed? Who does something similar or duplicates it? Should anyone specialise? Who has got the ability to cover in the case of sickness, absence, or a fluctuation in work?

How?

How? can be asked in two ways. One is to analyse each 'person' independently and look at his job as a whole. How related are the tasks of this person to others? How are his skills utilised? Is he spending 5 per cent of his time on something which he trained for, and 95 per cent of the time on some routine work which could be transferred elsewhere? How are his skills utilised? How repetitive are his tasks? How much checking or supervision is there? How many deadline or monotonous tasks? How heavy is his workload? It is becoming progressively more and more important to give people authority and responsibility in their work, to give them job interest and to give them what appears to them a fair crack of the whip.

The other use of how is to ask how is it performed? Except in the most simple operations, it is a good idea to do a simple block flow chart or diagram of the main steps in a procedure. Examples are given in Figs. 14.6 and 14.7. After you have prepared a block chart of the procedure you can then apply critical analysis to it again, as critical analysis always yields an additional set of results as one looks at each procedure in more detail.

There is nothing done so well that it cannot be done better, or more simply, or more sensibly. By asking the critical analysis sequence about different steps in the procedure, one will find that there are many activities which are either unnecessary, or if necessary, are not cost effective. Costs are changing all the time, particularly labour costs which have changed out of all proportion to other costs over the last few years. Assumptions made on the best evidence ten years ago may well not be valid today. In fact, who would say any assumptions made ten years ago would have been made in the same way if they had been reached under present conditions? In most areas you will find habits and procedures which have been in operation for much longer than that.

Job: Preparing an estimate (present method).

Chart begins with drawing and schedule in the sales department 'Out' basket, and ends with the completed estimate in the sales department 'In' basket

Man (Estimator)	*Material* (Estimate documentation)
Collects drawing and schedule from sales.	Drawing and schedule await collection by estimator.
Checks for completeness etc.	To estimator's desk.
Goes to price files.	Checked for completeness etc.
Notes prices on schedule.	To price files.
Returns to desk.	Priced by estimator.
Extends and totals prices.	To estimator's desk.
Prepares two-part estimate form.	Schedule totalled and extended.
Files second copy estimate with drawing and schedule.	Two-part estimate form prepared.
Takes top copy of estimate to sales.	Second copy estimate filed with drawing and schedule.
	Top copy estimate to sales department.

Explanation of symbols:

operation predominant characteristic 'does', 'adds to', 'creates'.

inspection or checking.

transportation - predominant characteristic 'moves'.

delay which is part of the processor procedure.

storage or filing.

Fig. 14.6 Flow process charts – 'man' type
and 'material' type

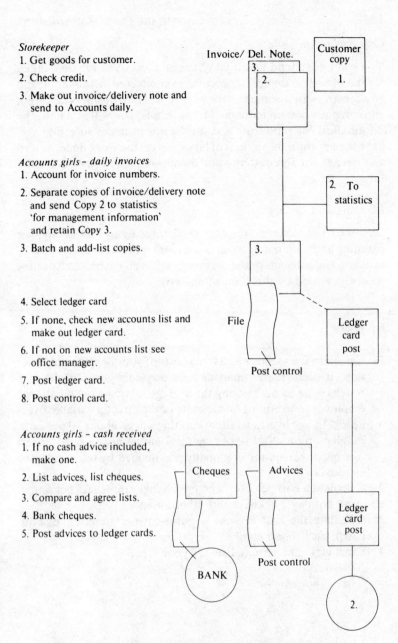

Storekeeper
1. Get goods for customer.
2. Check credit.
3. Make out invoice/delivery note and send to Accounts daily.

Invoice/ Del. Note.

Customer copy

Accounts girls – daily invoices
1. Account for invoice numbers.
2. Separate copies of invoice/delivery note and send Copy 2 to statistics 'for management information' and retain Copy 3.
3. Batch and add-list copies.

2. To statistics

4. Select ledger card
5. If none, check new accounts list and make out ledger card.
6. If not on new accounts list see office manager.
7. Post ledger card.
8. Post control card.

File

Post control

Ledger card post

Accounts girls – cash received
1. If no cash advice included, make one.
2. List advices, list cheques.
3. Compare and agree lists.
4. Bank cheques.
5. Post advices to ledger cards.

Cheques

Advices

Ledger card post

BANK

Post control

Fig. 14.7 Flowchart of simple Sales and Accounts procedure

Cost evaluation

You will understand that if you have an analysis of the time taken for the various activities or procedures conducted in your area, and you can know or assume the volumes or levels of business involved, you can put a cost on individual transactions; you will also have the information for producing a control form to make sure that you have the appropriate amount of labour to get the work done, as well as a means for forecasting your manpower requirements for the future.

Planning and control

Chapter 16 describes methods of using these figures for manpower planning and labour control and goes into more detail as to how to evaluate and account for the performance levels of your staff as they will be revealed by this kind of analysis.

Exercises

1   Calculate the variable and fixed costs of your department/function. If there are no management accounts you can obtain a rough figure by multiplying the average salary by the number of employees and adding an estimate of the directly variable overheads. In low overhead situations this will be about 70 per cent, ranging up to 120–130 per cent in London head offices. Fixed overheads can be taken globally and divided by the number of employees.
2   Calculate a cost per hour and minute per employee, bearing in mind holidays, sickness and other absences.
3   Calculate the cost in your department per transaction, unit, batch, etc., if you can.
4   Draft task and activity lists for your area.

15 Causes of difference in output

'*A man came to bathe in a river. He thought the water would be cool and refreshing. But instead he found an ocean with roaring waves. He was frightened.*'

Prafulla Mohanti

The manager does not want to waste the labour of his staff, one of the most expensive and scarce resources under his control. We all want to operate at maximum effectiveness by planning to keep our subordinates occupied with useful work. So, we have to assess the work content of our procedures, and we have to assess the capacity of our employees. Both may vary; the amount of work to be done will alter, and the output of our staff will change.

This chapter aims to provide a checklist of the factors which can cause a change in output or rate of working, and which may explain differences in performance. To understand and plan the output of our staff we will want to consider these factors, whether intuitively or systematically. They are illustrated in diagrammatic form in Fig. 15.1.

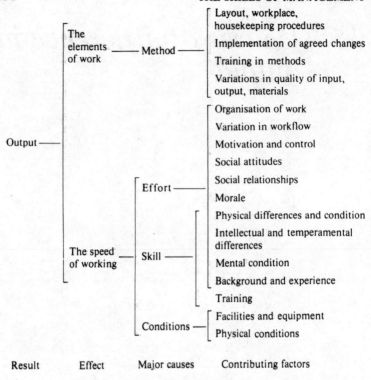

Result   Effect   Major causes   Contributing factors

Fig. 15.1 Causes of difference in output

Methods

It is generally found that incorrect methods are the main depressing influence on output. Under the heading of methods are included:

1 Layout
2 Workplace
3 Housekeeping
4 Procedures
5 Implementation of changes
6 Training in methods

In order to control the work of a section, department or branch, we have to agree a method for doing that work. Sometimes staff will improve on the specified method, but in general, departure from the method will involve additional elements of work which increase the time taken.

Layout and workplace organisation

If performance falls below the expected level the manager should check whether the layout and workplace organisation are as agreed, and whether the 'housekeeping' is as good as was envisaged. He should check whether there are any agreed methods changes that have to be implemented. He should check whether the staff know and follow the agreed methods, and consider whether he and his seniors are spending enough time in training the others in those methods.

Unnecessary actions

He may find that unnecessary actions have crept in, or that work is being done over which there could be a difference of opinion. An example of this is 'rechecking' of references or calculations to 'make sure'. The manager must then decide if the rechecking serves a valid purpose, i.e. are errors picked up, and is the cost of those errors such as to justify the recheck?

Other determining factors

If, however, the procedures and layout are substantially as agreed, the supervisor will have to look further; he may be aware, of course, of other determining factors before he looked at the procedures. These will fall into two categories: other considerations affecting methods, and those which bear on the actual performance of the individual staff and the section as a whole. The former are variations in quality of input, output and materials.

Variations in the nature and quality of documents and source data

Such variations might or might not affect the detail of the procedures but often affect the proportions of one element to another. In general, these variations would fall into one or more of the following categories, and these could be checked by sampling:

(a)   a different 'mix';
(b)   variation in form;
(c)   variation in content;
(d)   variation in legibility;
(e)   variation in error-rate;
(f)   variation in flow.

Quality of output

The same sort of considerations apply to the quality of output as affect quality of input. The quality of work in the section may go up or down, and while the basic procedures remain unchanged, the detailed methods will be found to have altered.

Variations in quality of materials

These can have a major effect in production and maintenance areas. It may well be that a change in supply or in buying specification has taken place without the manager being informed. Small changes in specification of office stationery and consumables are less likely to be significant; changes such as from carbon interleaving to snap-out sets for correspondence would fall into the category of methods changes, and in the field of machine operation, particularly with printing, collating, and photocopying machines, a change in paper or materials may result in the equipment being run at a higher speed than that previously accepted as normal. Less suitable materials would result of course in reduced performance. It should be noted that the supplier may have changed the specification, with or without notice, and the supervisor might not be aware of the change.

Effort

Even if the methods are correct, the required standard of effort, skill, or conditions may not be met. The manager should check the following points to see whether he needs to take action. (See Fig. 15.1.)

Organisation of work

Recognition must be given to the fact that repetition of operations leads to different levels of speeds resulting from special skills, and that a higher average performance results when staff can settle down to a regular repetitive operation, such as occurs, for example, on production lines.

In general, one cannot fully achieve this smooth rhythmic motion pattern that can be characteristic of the production line, but there may be opportunities for moving towards this kind of approach. By batching work, and by applying the principles of motion economy, very large improvements in productivity (frequently of the order of

50 per cent) can be achieved. Likewise, it follows that if the work-flow is such that staff can never settle down to their tasks, and never know from one minute to the next what will happen, performance will suffer. Disorganisation often results from interruptions or 'queries'.

Suggestions
The action to be taken will vary from situation to situation, but some suggestions are as follows:

1 Split up the work so that each worker can concentrate on one job for a worthwhile period.
2 Avoid general access to departmental staff from outside.
3 In the event of large quantities of outside calls or callers, detail staff to deal with these (possibly in rotation) so as to leave the rest free to concentrate on other work. Do not have more outside phone points working than you wish to 'man'.
4 Discourage personal visits. Try to restrict access to the department to specified times or on specified conditions.
5 Try to batch 'queries' and avoid lengthy searches while the caller waits. If proper 'phone-back' arrangements are made, a great deal of time can be saved. Internal queries should be by note if practicable, and a notepad and pencil suitably placed by the entrance to the department can be useful. (It is remarkable how many queries seem to answer themselves if the enquirer tries to formulate the question in writing.)
6 Analyse the interruptions and try to have them dealt with at first hand by the most appropriate person. Try not, however, to have yourself (the manager or supervisor) bogged-down into a sort of superior query clerk.

From a general point of view the manager should attempt to determine what the work content, and therefore cost, of the operations, transactions or procedure is, and what is the average performance. If an appropriate work measurement scheme has been installed this will make assessment simpler, but there are other methods such as sampling, estimating and time-logging (diary sheets), which can give a useful indication.

Raising performances
Performances above or below the average should be seen for what

they are, and the reasons for variations should be sought and kept under review. Once the cost of below-average performance is determined, it is much easier to make decisions about the factors which may be causing it. The manager should be striving continually to raise the performance in his area to an acceptable level by enthusiastic leadership, and by the removal of obstacles to even higher output by better methods and better practice.

Variation in workflow

The manager should make every effort to see that work is fairly distributed and that employees are not kept waiting for work. He will know that periods of inactivity are bad for morale, and that it may be difficult to restore a proper working tempo if there are too many gaps. We know that in certain circumstances unavoidable troughs will occur which cannot be filled by special jobs, loaning-out, or other expedients. The manager should calculate the effect of these troughs as accurately as possible and target accordingly (see also Chapter 6). At the very least he will become aware of the cost and effects of the variability of the workflow, and alive to opportunities for reducing it as and when they occur.

Motivation and control

We see here a major role of the supervision. It is most desirable to encourage delegation of authority and responsibility to the lowest practicable level, and it is equally important to be cost and innovation conscious, and fully in control of the work and our employees. Some of the underlying factors affecting personal output are discussed below.

Social attitudes

Output will be affected by social attitudes in certain cases. Political attitudes can be important; for instance, a person who does not believe in the capitalist system will not have the same attitude to the commercial problems of the enterprise as one convinced of the necessity of competition and the profit motive. Someone who believes the economy is sound and expanding will view change and effort differently from one who sees it as static or declining. Likewise, a highly religious or sensitive person may recoil from red-blooded purchasing and selling work or bad debt recovery procedures. Traditionalists may be upset if, for example, personal letters are replaced by a stereotyped form.

History

History plays a part too. In an area where unemployment, business crashes, or hire and fire have been experienced people will react differently from a place where respectable and prosperous employers have competed for the available labour for as long as anyone can remember. The history of the company itself will play an important part.

Constructive and confident attitude

The manager must adopt a constructive and confident attitude, and should attempt to reconcile the individual's view with his work and with the policy of the company or organisation. He should be ready to demonstrate the relevance of the work to the future of the individual, group, company, community, or country as appropriate. This enthusiasm will eventually rub off on the others, and even if he makes no converts, the staff will respect him better if they feel he understands their beliefs and feelings and is prepared to discuss them.

Groups

Groups are not the same as individuals; groups will adopt certain attitudes and tempos of work, and their members will tend to conform when in the group situation. It should be considered whether an improvement can be obtained by making it possible for trouble-makers and misfits to be transferred to where they would be more useful.

Morale

Morale is an amalgam of all the points mentioned in this chapter. We believe that if staff can be shown that they are playing a valuable and valued part in a successful and respected enterprise, and that they are using their talents in the best way to benefit both themselves and their employer, they will respond in a remarkable way.

Remember also that the progress of any organisation is like the battle of Waterloo, 'a damned close-run thing'. After one has been in any company for a few years it becomes only too easy to see the last minute panics, the shifts and devices, the personal failings and the mistakes. The thing is to keep on trying, at least you will win some of the time.

Personal differences
One would expect that in an organisation with proper selection procedures, wage structures and job grading and promotion arrangements, the staff recruited will be of at least 'average' calibre and will be trained and placed in a satisfactory manner.

Quality of employees
However, even allowing for a percentage of mistakes, one is often surprised at how many complaints are made about the 'quality' of employees. Sometimes this is a case of the bad workman blaming his tools – there are no bad men, only bad officers. A manager who criticises his staff may well be really saying, 'I am unable to get these people to do what I want'. Perhaps also there are few really bad 'officers', but many managers and supervisors do not have sufficient training – they do not have the tools for the job, and it is the aim of this book to help in this respect.

Social relationships and behaviour

We have considered the effect on individual members of staff of various factors and relationships. We know that the individuals' needs for recognition and inclusion are affected by relationships with:

(a)   other staff;
(b)   supervision;
(c)   management;
(d)   family;
(e)   other people outside the company.

There is no need to elaborate on these points.

Behaviour of people
What, however, is surprising sometimes is the apparent contradiction between the behaviour of a person when on his own and when in a group, e.g. at a meeting. This can be quite confusing as, for instance, when a person accepts a proposed change in private and then argues against it later, or alternatively when he refuses to have anything to do with a certain line of thinking and then warmly supports it at the next meeting. Often this may be no more than a

subconscious or semi-deliberate device to gain time to sort the matter out or discuss it elsewhere. Sometimes it may be a question of 'positions'. The manager, foreman, supervisor or staff may have adopted a certain position on the procedures or operation of the section and feel they cannot go back on this in front of each other without loss of face. They may have no entrenched position but feel that they have to assert themselves by taking a certain line even in spite of their own reasoning. It may be that in a situation where the natural nervousness or diffidence of an individual are brought out, he may retreat from a proposal he is not absolutely certain of.

Staff as a group
The same sort of considerations apply in dealing with the staff as a group, e.g. in talks or discussions. Most groups subconsciously throw up a spokesman, and this person can be most useful in gaining the staff's co-operation. Obviously the foreman or supervisor is the local spokesman but he has to work on the situation as he finds it.

Leadership
A leader uses example, persuasion and compulsion to make people do what they would otherwise be disinclined or unable to perform. Leadership involves an understanding of people, their strengths and weaknesses, their hopes and fears, and we will proceed now to attempt to summarise these factors so that we can know better why individuals perform and act in different ways.

Physical differences

Physical differences and physical skills are more important in manual working situations. Most office work requires no special physical effort or abilities and given training normal differences of age, sex physique and left and right handedness are not too greatly significant in themselves. Extremes of age and youth or dexterity and clumsiness would affect results but the manager should have no difficulty in recognising this.

Disabled or handicapped persons
Actually disabled or handicapped persons are at a disadvantage, although this can often be minimised, i.e. by giving a legless man a completely sedentary job. By law (Disabled Persons Employment Acts, 1944 and 1958) any establishment with over twenty workers

must employ 3 per cent of disabled persons under the Acts, or be willing to. This is still in force.

Just as in the case of trainees, the supervisor will determine what he can expect, i.e. 50 per cent, 75 per cent of the norm or whatever is appropriate, and target accordingly. Considerations of policy and charity affect these matters, but it may be shown that in the case of handicapped or misfits it may be cheaper and kinder to pay for a 'golden handshake' or an early pension than to continue employing them. In any case it should be made clear to all such persons that none of them would be pressed to perform at more than their capacity. Most supervisors know that it is counterproductive to ask too much of their subordinates.

Physical condition

Physical condition in employees is important. It is not necessary for them to be athletically 'fit' (this may even be a disadvantage in a sedentary occupation), but workers should be reasonably fresh and alert throughout the day. Unfitness leads to absence, fellow-travelling and often to a grudging attitude to work. Physical condition may be affected by ventilation, lighting, cramped conditions, etc., which are within the employer's control.

Other factors which affect fitness for work include:

1 Moonlighting (evening and weekend jobs).
2 Excessive social commitments (particularly with young people).
3 Heavy domestic commitments (e.g. the patter of tiny feet, moving house, looking after relatives, etc.).
4 Outside activities (e.g. local council work, etc.).
5 Difficult commuting.
6 Alcoholism.
7 Inadequate feeding – female staff frequently miss breakfast and have a skimped lunch. This leads to loss of concentration in the afternoon.

The company may have a policy on these points and on bad sickness records, but in general the manager can only accept these factors and judge accordingly (in his official capacity at least).

Intellectual and temperamental differences

It can be useful to realise that there are intellectual and temperamental differences in people, and to use this knowledge in harnessing their abilities in the most effective way. It may help to understand apparently inexplicable contradictions in behaviour and performance. It is not within the compass of this book to consider in detail the range of temperamental and intellectual make-up, but as with physical characteristics, otherwise suitably equipped persons can be reduced to a low pitch of performance and concentration if they are not mentally fit.

Mental condition

We cannot go into the question of disorders of the mind and nervous system and mental breakdowns, although the incidence of this type of illness is increasing. It may be possible to see something is wrong because the person suffers a deep depression or behaves as if he is 'off his rocker'. What, however, we are much more likely to encounter is:

1 Preoccupation. Worries over domestic problems, e.g., spouse, sweetheart, children, money, will all distract people.
2 Shock. Tragic experiences like deaths, seeing an accident, etc., may throw employees off their form for a period.
3 Tiredness. This is linked with the points of physical fitness. A tired body can house an alert mind and vice versa, but generally a lack of mental energy will accompany a lack of physical energy.

Background and experience

The extent to which an individual can control and direct his mental abilities and temperamental characteristics is much influenced by background, education, and experience. The basic mental horsepower or I.Q. of the individual does not develop much after the age of sixteen, but powers of concentration, flexibility of approach and development of abilities can be improved until the individual is in his late forties or fifties. In many cases a person who can make good use of a limited I.Q. can put up a better performance than a person of higher I.Q. but less mental discipline. In clerical work one must look to match the individual to the work. Too good a mind will become frustrated and dull; too limited an intelligence will become strained.

Training

One of the most obvious causes of difference in output is the degree
and quality of training and of experience. Targeting of performance
will be set by the manager and supervisor in the light of this, and
they will be aware of the cost of staff turnover on the one hand and
of the necessity for careful training on the other. By demonstration,
and by using whatever aids he can obtain or produce, e.g. charts,
diagrams and checklists, the manager will ensure that each employee understands the agreed methods and procedures in detail, and
will watch to see these procedures are followed (until better ones
are developed). See Chapter 13 for a discussion of teaching and
training methods.

It need hardly be said that short interval scheduling figures and
standards (where available) can be a valuable aid in assessing the
progress of trainees.

Conditions

Facilities and equipment

It is as well to check the following points:

1 Are furniture and fixtures of proper height and size – are they
   limiting the work in any way?
2 Is there enough space for orderly storage?
3 Do drawers and doors open properly and do they interfere
   with other operations?
4 Are the seats properly adjusted and comfortable?
5 Is all equipment functioning properly? Are there suitable
   maintenance arrangements?
6 Do the relevant staff understand the use of the equipment?
7 Are materials and tools placed for easiest access and disposal?

Physical conditions

Physical conditions and environment will affect the rate of working
and in some cases the methods. Good work performances can be
obtained in all except extreme conditions but the following points
should be noted.

Light
Natural light should fall over the left shoulder or come from the left (for right handed operations), and staff should not face a window. Direct or reflected glare and excessive variations in brightness should be avoided. A higher level of illumination is required for machine work.

Heat
The temperature should be controlled within the range of 66–70°F.

Ventilation
Too much of a 'fug' will lead to concentration of carbon dioxide in the air and to sleepy and unhealthy conditions. Odours and smoke should be cleared without causing draughts.

Noise
Most people can get used to a steady hum but are distracted by intermittent noise. A high noise level is tiring and can be reduced by acoustic tiling, screening, double-glazing, and soft floor coverings, e.g. cork tiles or carpets.

Space
Minimum standards are laid down in the Offices, Shops, and Railway Premises Act 1963 (40 sq. ft. average where ceiling height is 10 ft or more, 400 cu. ft. otherwise). In most expanding companies space is in short supply, as well as being expensive, but workers do feel better when they can move freely about and do not feel 'hemmed in' at their places of work. Supervision too, is easier in areas which are laid out with more than the bare minimum of space.

Environment
The general standard of decor, machines, equipment and furniture, and of restroom, cloakroom, canteen, car park facilities and the like will often fall outside the immediate responsibility of the manager, although these matters will almost certainly be raised by the employees with him. The manager may attend meetings or have other occasions where he can put forward recommendations, either on his own or in conjunction with other proposals.

The manager cannot measure the effect of poor environment or physical conditions, but he will know that changes in them will cause differences in output. He should acquire copies of the relevant legislation concerning physical conditions. The Acts concerned make heavy reading, but guides are published by HMSO and some industrial training boards.

1   Health and Safety at Work Act 1974.
2   Fire Precautions Act 1971.
3   Offices, Shops and Railway Premises Act 1963.
4   Factories Act 1961.

Performance

We have considered a wide variety of factors which could lead to performance falling below (or in rarer cases, exceeding) a reasonable standard. Many of these factors are of vital interest to management and supervision in a wider context than work performances. Most of them imply a requirement of personal knowledge of people and work situation in each section which is in itself, probably the first step to achieving effective management.

Exercises

1   Identify three occasions on which output has varied from what you expected. Attempt to analyse the reasons for this.
2   Identify one member of your staff who produces better results than you would have expected. What are the reasons for this, and would they be relevant to any of the others?
3   Identify one member of your staff who produces worse results than he should. What are the reasons for this and can you do anything about them? Might these factors affect any other staff?
4   Are there any occasions when you feel you cannot give of your best? Why is this, and would the reasons be applicable to any other staff? Is this likely to happen more frequently or less frequently?

16 Manpower planning and control

' "You always rise twice" he said
Is no consolation to a man that thinks to drown.'

A.L. Rowse

In Chapter 14 we looked at a simple method of obtaining a ratio or relationship between the work to be done and the labour required. There are various ways of doing this, and this chapter assumes that you have obtained this basic data and want to consider ways of using it for planning and control.

Performance and progress report

There are various forms which can be used, a very common one being known as the performance and progress report; a more complex version of this form which can assist in manpower planning is given in Fig. 16.1.

Mechanics of the form

Basis of plan
The mechanics of the preparation of this form are as follows. In the

Part 1. Output. Page of   Division/Dept. ....   Branch ....   Section ....

Basis of plan

Activity	Volume	PERIOD 1		PERIOD 2		PERIOD 3		PERIOD 4		PERIOD 5		PERIOD 6		TOTAL
		Planned	Actual	Planned	Actual	Planned	Actual	Planned	Actual	Planned	Actual	Planned	Actual	
1.														
2.														
3.														
4.														
5.														
6.														
7.														
8.														
9.														
Activity	*Unit time*													
1.														
2.														
3.														
4.														
5.														
6.														
7.														
8.														
9.														
Subtotal														
B/F from page														
Total														
Man hours required														
Regular work														
Special work														
Service work														
Total														
Adjustments made to performance level, if any + %														

Fig. 16.1 Manpower plan

Part 2. Input. Page of   Division/Dept. ....   Branch ....   Section ....

C. Proposed number of staff

	PERIOD 1		PERIOD 2		PERIOD 3		PERIOD 4		PERIOD 5		PERIOD 6		TOTAL
	Planned	Actual	Planned	Actual	Planned	Actual	Planned	Actual	Planned	Actual	Planned	Actual	
Permanent													
Temporary													
Total													
Supervision													

D. Man hours provided

	PERIOD 1		PERIOD 2		PERIOD 3		PERIOD 4		PERIOD 5		PERIOD 6		TOTAL
	Planned	Actual	Planned	Actual	Planned	Actual	Planned	Actual	Planned	Actual	Planned	Actual	
Permanent staff:													
(i) - bank holiday													
(ii) - sickness													
(iii) - leave													
(iv) - training													
(v) Subtotal													
(vi) loaning out													
(vii) + borrowing													
(viii) + overtime													
Temporary staff:													
(ix) Net staff													
Hours required (from Part 1)													
Surplus													
+ leave													
Maximum leave capability.													

Fig. 16.1 (continued)

'basis of plan' box put in the company plan, marketing plan, or source data, which may be estimates from examination of historical figures which you used to look ahead in planning your manpower.

Volume
Under the column 'volume' we would enter the activities as determined in producing the work distribution chart in lines 1 to 9. If the operations exceed 9, obviously one would use additional sheets or a form designed with more lines on it. Then enter the forecast volumes of all operations by period and cross cast to annual totals.

Unit time
Periods will vary from company to company as appropriate, depending on the accounting or management information arrangements. In some cases it may be by calendar month, in other cases four-week periods or quarters. Under the 'unit time' column insert the time for each procedure or transaction or unit as established from the work distribution chart. If you have not already done this, all that is required is to divide the total time, for example that spent on processing invoices, by the number of invoices processed during the period. Then multiply the volumes by the times for each period rounding to the nearest hour, and into extensions in the relevant boxes. Add these up to given period totals of hours. If more than one sheet has to be used, total all sheets and carry forward totals to sheet 1, and then enter these figures on part two of the form.

Hours required
In the last section of the form, which is described as 'hours required' there are three sections. One is hours required for any special work such as budget preparation, year end accounts, or stock takings, and sometimes you may wish to add extra hours for service levels. What is meant here is, for example, the case of a counter in a bank, a check-in area, or a booking office, where it may be necessary to provide a greater number of clerks in order to facilitate an agreed level of service, regardless of the actual amount of work.

The amount of work will fluctuate during the year, and obviously it is one of the purposes of the exercise to show and quantify this variation. The performance of people against the differing volumes should be normally a constant ratio, except where there are seasonal effects on the characteristics of the work. In the latter case there may be two or more levels of performance during the year, but periodic variations in work volumes should not in themselves cause fluctuations in the unit times. What can occur, however, is an improvement or deterioration in the level of performance for other reasons.

Effective utilisation of time

It is normally found that when some sort of control or target is applied to the actual effectiveness of the staff, then effective utilisation of time improves. It is impossible to be specific about this, but the general situation in an 'uncontrolled' area is that performances are something like 60 per cent of optimum; by the use of the type of techniques mentioned in the book, and by controls one can increase productivity by 20 to 30 per cent. It follows that any movement in that direction would influence the calculations involved in estimating the requirement for future periods or months.

The next step is to determine the basic permanent staff numbers, and you will need to use part two of your manpower planning form. The object of this is to match, as closely as is reasonable, the net staff hours which are shown at the bottom of the section 'Man hours provided' with the hours required from the bottom of part one. There will be a degree of trial and error before the final level of staff and overtime can be determined.

Man hours provided

A base figure is required to start the calculations. Enter this at the top and extend it to give the permanent staff gross attendance hours in each period, and enter these figures on the first line of the 'man hours provided' section. (The present or expected permanent staff numbers multiplied by the normal working hours per period will give the gross attendance hours.)

Permanent staff — bank holidays

In addition to annual leave, public holidays should be added in the appropriate period.

Permanent staff — sickness

Estimate expected absence through sickness, taking into account likely seasonal variations, and enter these in the appropriate periods. Average sickness per employee in excess of two weeks per year should be recorded as worthy of further investigation.

Annual leave
Enter expected or planned figures.

Training programme
Enter expected or planned figures.

Subtotal
Deduct holidays, sickness, leave, and training from permanent staff attendance hours. The resulting balance, at this point in the completion of the forms, will give the present anticipated provision of permanent staff time, period by period. These figures should be compared with the period totals of required hours to show shortfalls or exercises requiring adjustment in the following manner.

Training and leave
The first step towards obtaining any extra time on a period by period basis is to consider whether any training or leave, at present allocated in periods where shortfalls occur, can be further regulated. Make any possible adjustments and re-compare to see whether shortfalls still exist.

Borrowing and loaning-out of time
The next step is to explore with the other managers the availability of surplus staff time in other sections or branches having appropriate skills. In the event that arrangements can be made to borrow time, enter the amounts for each period. Separate lines can be used to show sections from which the time has been borrowed. If there is a surplus in your own function, then the reverse process should be adopted.

Temporary staff
If the time made available by borrowing does not meet the shortfall, or if borrowing is not practicable, the possibility of recruiting temporary staff for the required periods should be considered, and if arrangements can be made the time they will contribute should be entered in the appropriate line.

Overtime

Any remaining shortfalls should be met by overtime to the extent that local agreements allow, and only as far as is reasonable, and, of course, providing the economics are viable and demonstrable. However, if at this stage it is apparent that the shortfalls in any period or periods cannot be met practically and economically by borrowed time, temporary staff and overtime, it then becomes necessary to go back to the beginning of the first section and to draw up a new plan based on additional staff numbers. This may, of course, include either permanent employees or seasonal and part-time workers recruited at the appropriate time to meet needs. These extra staff should be added only to the extent necessary to reach the minimum of man hours required after borrowing and the use of temporary staff and overtime opportunities have been explored fully.

Addition of columns

The addition of the columns will now give planned net staff hours available, and these should again be compared with the period totals of required hours to show any surplus hours available. If there are surplus hours, then these should be offered as far as practicable to the other sections or branches in the organisation or be used for any other necessary work. (Subject to the considerations outlined in the next paragraph.) If arrangements are made to lend any surplus time, enter the amounts period by period; separate lines can be used to show the sections to which the staff have been loaned. Then complete the period columns to give net attendance hours, cross cast all lines to give annual totals.

Monthly surpluses

At the bottom of the form are columns for monthly surpluses. It may be necessary and desirable to have some surplus in reserve to provide for the effects of partly trained staff, disabled staff, temporary fluctuations, or for any other reason. However, this figure should not be too high, as the figures obtained from the work distribution chart represent levels of effectiveness related to the present situation.

Planning and scheduling purposes

The completed form and the figures obtained from the work distribution chart can be used also for planning and scheduling purposes, and Chapter 6 should be considered in conjunction with results at this time. You have now a valuable tool to assist in short term staff planning and control. You have a means of justifying staff increases (or decreases) against estimated or actual changes in workload and business volumes.

Monthly performance control sheet

You will have appreciated that the form and system can be extended in detail or modified to show a variety of figures to help you in the management of your function. Examples of monthly 'control' sheets are given in Figs. 16.2, 16.3 and 16.4.

Valuable though this exercise of the preparation of manpower plan is, you will understand that it takes little account of the 'people', as distinct from the requirements of the work, and that a detailed approach of this kind could not be applied for more than a few months into the future. The problem of longer term manpower and succession planning can be looked at from an entirely different standpoint, and this is done by taking a 'stock' or 'inventory' of one's people, and by then comparing this with the company's requirements at different points in the future.

Longer term planning

The approach detailed next can be used for somewhere between 300 and 800 people as a maximum, because for larger numbers it is necessary to have a computer or other equipment to facilitate the movement of the data required. The approach must be modified to meet individual circumstances, but what is suggested is in essence as follows. Examine the jobs or positions in the organisation, or the senior posts in your own area. Once you have set out the situation in terms of job titles and numbers, consider then the kind of requirements which are needed for filling those various posts. Look then at the number of people you employ, who are already in your area, and consider whether they have the requirements to fill not only the

Department ....
Section ....
Month ....
Year ....

	Function/Task	Basis of assessment	Time	Month units	Time × units
MAN HOURS PROVIDED * 1. Permanent					
2. Temporary					
3. Borrowing					
4. Overtime					
5. TOTAL					
HOURS PAID FOR BUT NOT WORKED Bank Holidays					
Sickness					
Leave					
Training					
Other					
6. TOTAL					
7. Net hours worked (5-6)					
HRS PD BUT NOT SPENT ON MEASD WORK 8. Loaned out					
9. Special jobs (Unplanned or unexpected work)					
10. Net hours on normal work (7−[8+9])					
11. Net hours on measured wk % of total hours $\left(\frac{10\times100}{5}\right)$					
12. Workload. (Total of final column)					
13. Variance (12 v 10)					
14. EFFECTIVENESS $\left(\frac{12\times100}{10}\right)$					
15. Staff numbers					
16. Supervision					
17. Staff					

*Code figures refer to column numbers in the performance and progress report

Fig. 16.2 Monthly performance control sheet

| JOB SUMMARY OF STANDARD HOURS | | | | | | | |
| DEPARTMENT | | | | | DATE | | |
1 POSITION AND FUNCTIONS	2 BASIS OF MEASUREMENT	3 Unit Time	4 Actual Units	5 Work Hours	6 Actual Hours	7 Variance	8 % Effective
—	—	—	—	3×4	—	$6 - 5$	$\frac{5}{6} \times 100$
		(Time for transaction or procedure)					

Fig. 16.3 Another example of a control sheet

Company		Department		Section		Sheet No.											

Month and Year 19......	Man hours provided.									Net hrs. used on normal work	Net hrs. on normal work as % of total net hrs. wkd.	Workload (Times × units)	Variance	Effectiveness	Current staff numbers		Any relevant comments
	Permanent	Temporary	Borrowed	Overtime	Hrs. not worked (deduct)	Net hrs worked	Loaned (deduct)	Special jobs (deduct)						Supervision	Staff	
	1	2	3	4	6	7	8	9	10	11	12	13	14	16	17	
1																
2																
3																
4																
5																
6																
7																
8																
9																
10																
11																
12																
13																

Fig. 16.4 Example of a summary control sheet

MANPOWER PLANNING MATRIX

For period ____ Prepared by ____ Ref: ____ Date ____

AGE	*TIER I			*TIER II			*TIER III			*TIER IV			*TIER V			Total
	M	F	T	M	F	T	M	F	T	M	F	T	M	F	T	
64																
63																
62																
61																
60																
59																
58																
57																
56																
55																
54																
53																
52																
51																
50																
49																
48																
47																
46																
45																
44																
43																
42																
41																
40																

Fig. 16.5 Manpower planning matrix

MANPOWER PLANNING MATRIX

For period ____ Prepared by ____ Ref: ____ Date ____

AGE	*TIER I			*TIER II			*TIER III			*TIER IV			*TIER V			Total
	M	F	T	M	F	T	M	F	T	M	F	T	M	F	T	
39																
38																
37																
36																
35																
34																
33																
32																
31																
30																
29																
28																
27																
26																
25																
24																
23																
22																
21																
20																
19																
18																
17																
16																
Totals																

*Note – 'Tiers' are levels of ability or potential ability to fill different grades or ranks.

Fig. 16.6 Manpower planning matrix (continued)

positions which they are already filling, but also more senior or different posts. When you have done this complete a matrix.

Matrix

An example of a manpower planning matrix is shown in Figs. 16.5 and 16.6.

You will see that the matrix is set out in terms of the individuals' ages, because this is the one sure thing in all manpower planning – the inexorable (and regrettable!) march year by year towards retirement age. The matrix is divided also into male and female, because the career pattern and expectations of ladies are still different, even in this age of equal opportunity.

Other matrices can be made up for future years and situations, but for a quick look all one has to do is run a ruler down from the top of the matrix to blank out those who will have been lost to retirement in one to five years' time, or whatever the period selected; you can compare what remains with the expected requirement established for the year concerned. This may be the same as now, or it may be expanded or reduced in the expectation of the growth or attrition of the business or organisation.

One can see now whether any serious gaps in age structure are likely to occur, or whether there will be specific skills missing. One can look at the likely career progression of groups and individuals, and also forecast one's own prospects. (It is normal to obtain a clearer and more favourable view of the opportunities that are likely to turn up through doing this sort of exercise.) However, the analysis, conclusions, and use of these types of approaches will vary considerably from individual to individual depending on circumstances. What was intended in this chapter was to show two different mechanisms for producing base data for further analysis or managerial thinking, and for taking action to manage your department in a better way.

Exercises

This chapter requires much thought on your part. The exercise is to consider how the control and planning of your major resource, manpower, can be of value in your situation, and then to set about the matter.

An action or workplan is set out in the summary on p. 195.

17   The manager and the trade unions

'Verbal agreements aren't worth the paper they're written on.'
                                                    Sam Goldwyn

Introduction

The manager is expected to be good at everything; he is expected to
cope with a variety of relationships and pressures, from directors
and customers. This includes matters of profit and loss, income,
costs, plant and equipment, government legislation. In particular he
has to deal with his subordinates and in many cases this involves
contact and negotiation with union officials. This aspect of this task
can often take up a major proportion of his time – time which he
may grudge, as it takes him away from the many other matters he
should be coping with. What can he do about it?

I think it can be taken as axiomatic that not only are unions here
to stay, but also that groups of employees not hitherto 'unionised'
will become so. It can also be accepted that the unions themselves
will become better organised and more effective, and that local
representatives will be better directed and trained. Whether subsequent governments like it or not, the power derived fom the ability

to withhold labour in vital situations will have to be accepted as part of our national structure.

Shop stewards

The manager is not normally faced by 'the union' – he is faced by the local official, e.g. shop steward, convener, chapel father as the case may be.

Types of shop stewards

Shop stewards as we shall call them fall into three categories. Firstly, they are men with some managerial instincts and drive who have failed for one reason or another to become, or attempt to become managers themselves. These people find an outlet for their need for success and responsibility in union work. Secondly, they are men (or women) who are dedicated to the union and its ideals, and who really enjoy this type of work. Thirdly, they consist of reluctant heroes, men who are elected to the position because nobody else will take it or because their colleagues want them to be there. Some would say that there is a fourth category and these are persons who find it easier to do union work than to get on with the tasks they were originally hired to do, but I think this is a small and declining percentage.

The manager should identify which type of shop steward he has to deal with, but to recognise always that the union man is there to do a job and deserves as much courtesy and respect as any other colleague. The union official is a human being, and if he can withdraw your labour on one hand, or assist in the contribution of that labour on the other, then he is a very important person.

The shop steward is not subject to the same complex of pressures as the manager – and he does not require anything like the same abilities and training – but because he is concentrating on a few key tasks, basically protecting the rights of his members and securing as large a share of the cake as he can for them, he can be a formidable opponent. He may also be trained in negotiating to a superior level than the manager.

Pressures on shop stewards

You have attempted to find out what kind and calibre of man the shop steward is. Have a care also to evaluate the pressures on him, from his branch or committee, from his members (often very strong), and from his own ego. A union man's only criterion of success is what he achieves for his members; he has a strong personal need to strive for what they want and to be always pressing for something else, even if, as is often the case, and in times of government backed norms and ceilings, it is increased security and better treatment rather than just more money and benefits.

Profitability and communication

Some unions, for example the E.E.T.P.U., employ their own productivity experts who will point to ways in which profitability can be maintained or improved at the same time as wage levels are raised.

The stewards can be invaluable as a means of communication and negotiation with the workforce, and in policing fair personnel policies. If management and supervision work with them and not against them, union representatives can be good friends and sterling members of the industrial community.

Industrial action

However, in any human situation there will come a day when somebody says the wrong thing, breaks the rules or when management and union cannot agree. Where is the manager then? The steward can cause various disruptions, and these are, progressively:

(a)   overtime bans;
(b)   working to rule;
(c)   go slows;
(d)   wildcat strikes;
(e)   official strikes.

How did they happen? The most frequent cause of industrial action is lack of communication, whether real or imaginary, but other causes are:

(a)   differentials in pay;
(b)   other companies paying more;
(c)   work study rates;
(d)   conditions;
(e)   discipline.

Procedure agreement

Get some order into the situation. Come to a local or domestic procedure agreement with the union. This will be a comprehensive document which will lay down the rules for action in any industrial situation, whether over grievances, disputes, disciplinary procedures or claims.

The agreement will have to conform with the provisions of the Employment Protection Act 1975, and you may need to take advice on the interpretation of some of the sections in your own situation. The agreement will set out the reasons for industrial discipline, and it will define the relationships of the foreman, shop steward, management levels and workers. In particular, it will define the relationships and authority of the foreman, who is the primary representative of the company's policy on the shop floor, and who is normally involved in the first stages of any disciplinary actions and disputes with stewards and workers.

There is not enough space in a book of this nature to include a specimen agreement, and in any case what would be appropriate in one situation might be inappropriate in another, e.g. in matters of pay and seniority. However, all agreements will define the position regarding misconduct such as damage, stealing, constant bad timekeeping, drinking and aggressive behaviour, and at what point these transgressions merit verbal and written warnings and dismissal, by whom this can be done, and what arrangements there may be for appeal.

Grievance section

All agreements should have a grievance section, with a definition of grievances, a procedure and timescale for dealing with them, and an agreement not to down tools over a dispute until the grievance procedure has been exhausted.

Grievances include violations of the agreement, violation of safety laws or other legislation, or unjust treatment. Violations of the agreement might comprise arguments over seniority, overtime rates, job reclassification, transfers, replacements, promotions and pay scales. Unjust treatment of an employee might comprise matters such as personal discrimination, favouritism, excessive disciplining and punishment for violation of unposted rules.

A typical grievance clause in an agreement reads as follows: 'Grievance procedures may be instituted by an employee who alleges that he has been unfairly dealt with. Grievances may also be lodged by an employee who alleges the provisions of this contract have not been complied with'. Grievances should be lodged in writing and on a proper form. A sample form is shown in Fig. 17.1, but all forms should include: a brief description of the case; reference to the section of the agreement which is violated (if any); and the settlement wanted. The union may submit a grievance on its own behalf, and the shop steward or foreman may assist the employee in completing the form.

No agreement can cover every eventuality, although it can include a statement of policy as to treatment of matters not covered, and as to matters reserved entirely to management. Agreements should be 'fair', i.e. not pressing too heavily on the employees, nor yet giving them too much leverage *vis-à-vis* the company and their supervisors. Agreements must be signed by the company and the union(s), otherwise they will not be considered valid by an industrial tribunal, and they must be renewed regularly and re-signed, possibly as each yearly wage bargaining is negotiated.

Ways to avoid possible confrontations

So what do we do to try and avoid getting caught in a situation where we have allowed unreasonable requests to arise, and where we have as an alternative to a costly and nerve-wracking dispute, loss of face and an expensive and precedent-creating capitulation?

Joint consultation procedure

Keep in touch by having a joint consultation procedure whereby material changes in conditions, machinery, systems, etc., can be discussed with the stewards, and where impending complaints and claims can be brought up by the union 'side'. These meetings can provide an opportunity for improvement in communications, i.e. when the company's progress and future plans can be presented and discussed. Consultation meetings should be held at least quarterly, and there should be provision for either side to request an emergency meeting.

```
┌─────────────────────────────────────────────────────────────┐
│ Name of                                        Time card      │
│ aggrieved employee _____ No. _____  │
│ Dept./Section _____ │
│ Employee's statement of grievance _____ │
│ _____ │
│ _____ │
│ _____ │
│ _____ │
│ _____ │
│ _____ │
│ Signature                         Signature                   │
│ of employee _____ of steward _____ │
│ Date presented to foreman ____ / ____ / _____ Department ___ │
│ Foreman's answer _____ │
│ _____ │
│ _____ │
│ _____ │
│                                   Signature                   │
│ Date _____ of foreman _____ │
│ Date to grievance committee ____ / ____ / _____ Chairman ___ │
│ _____ │
│ _____ │
│ _____ │
└─────────────────────────────────────────────────────────────┘
```

Fig. 17.1 Grievance form

Sensible or fair pay structure

Job evaluation and grading systems which are clearly understood and accepted are a major factor in avoiding industrial troubles. An experienced negotiator suggested that the best way is to fix the top and bottom pay on market considerations, and then to let the grading committee (on which the management side should be a minority) sort out what happens in between.

Undertaking or agreement on security of employment

The spectre of redundancies, lay-offs, short time, or sackings of any kind increases any existing distrust between labour and management, as well it might. Perhaps you cannot guarantee perpetual employment, but at least have a clear and written agreement about the proper consultations and procedures which covers what would happen if there was a major downturn in business or a change in plans.

Policy on pay and productivity

Many disputes over pay arise because managements have made no clear (or open) plans for increasing pay and other benefits. Considerable thought is given to improving profitability and productivity, little to how much of the cake is to be passed out. Labour learns that the only way to get a pay rise is to ask for one, and pretty soon after follow that with threats and action. A Pavlovian response is created, i.e. no strike = small increase, strike = bigger increase. Perhaps the moderate, the average union member, does not want to strike for many reasons as it not only hurts the company, it also hurts his pocket while it happens, but he begins to learn that only by screwing management can he get a reasonable deal.

Decide on your objectives

In any negotiations over wages and conditions, management should have in mind what it is prepared to pay and to concede before starting. This final situation may well be expressed as a number of alternatives, e.g. basic pay, overtime, holiday and shift allowances, working hours, breaks, productivity deals. The company will not offer all alternatives at the outset, just as the union(s) will probably make initial claims in excess of the figure they feel they would finally settle for. This is the normal process of any bargaining, and as each side adjusts to the other so a compromise is reached which is seen as the best that could be obtained under the circumstances. It is important for management to try and avoid a position in which either side has no further flexibility – one in which union negotiators backed by an angry committee and angry members feel that there is no point in continuing talks, and that they must proceed to industrial action. Try always to explain why the company is taking a particular line or offering a particular figure.

When disputes occur

These things will help, but there will still be disputes. When money is the subject you can never satisfy everyone, and someone at some stage is bound to make a mistake. When it comes to the showdown remember a few points.

Always tell the truth

Respect any agreements and try not to make 'deals' regarding their provisions. If the company is in the wrong admit it, back down and apologise. If there is some doubt, it may be better to give in than see the business halted, but one should not give in over everything. If an issue is clear-cut, and there is no major contingent hazard in taking a stand at a particular time, fight and win your fight. In a manufacturing business with a full warehouse and a dip in sales, or on a construction site during a spell of bad weather, every employee on strike will be saving you maybe £15 a day in wages, so the cards are not always stacked on one side. However, if you do make a stand, either on this basis, or when an angry steward bursts in on you, make sure you are in the right.

Contravening the procedure agreement

Trade union men, particularly full-time officials, uphold procedures and rules, and this is one reason for having a local procedure agreement. If a steward contravenes the agreed procedures, you may be able to bring pressure to bear through the full-time or branch official. Having said that though, be well aware that any agreement is only a piece of paper; both sides should observe it, but faced with a group of angry men or an unexpected situation, the union man may feel unable to stick to what has been agreed, perhaps under quite different circumstances.

Avoiding confrontation

Another tip is to try to take the dispute out of a management/labour confrontation. Unions are aware that their demands increase costs, although they feel that in the long run cost pressure forces management to increase efficiency and investment and hence productivity. If negotiations over rates can be translated into the estimating or quoting area, and into higher prices, so that both sides can see the effect of higher prices or costs on future business, then common sense is more likely to obtain.

Summary

Once things start to hot up, play it by the book. Do not panic or be stampeded into quick decisions, unless 'they' are in the right, when you should concede as graciously as possible. Once 'they' are out, they are losing money. Be firm and watch them change, but keep some concessions available so that the stewards can recommend a return to work without losing face.

Summary and workplan

'There's a tiresome young man in Bay Shore,
When his fiancée cried: "I adore
The beautiful sea!"
He replied: "I agree,
It's pretty, but what is it for?"'

Morris Bishop

Congratulations! Either you have ploughed through the book or else you have skipped to the end to see whether it was worth your while to read all the contents. Either way you have reached the point of summary. What did the book contain? What message did it preach? What must I do now?

Each chapter has its own suggestions, and most of them their own exercises. But what follows is a form on which you can enter in your own specific action plans. Now, do not try to do too much – or you will stop in frustration. I do not know what would be too much for you, but for me I try to do one constructive item in addition to routine each day. I have been doing this for years and I am so conditioned now that I get a guilty feeling if for any reason I miss out.

Your plan must be desirable, achievable, and specific. I keep emphasising this word 'specific', because less specific objectives, e.g. 'improve communications', 'have a look at the property market', 'cut down on expenses', tend to open too big an area to be satisfactorily tackled in the normal course of events – they are too general to prompt specific actions to be scheduled in with the other work. But you know all that by now, and you can either use the plan form given or make your own. The plan has five columns.

(a) Objective. Under each chapter heading we have entered the exercises and activities proposed, and left space for actions you intend to take which are particular to your own area or function.

(b) How it is to be achieved. What plan or method are you going to use?

(c) When is it to be started? Who is to be involved, will it be you alone, or will colleagues, superiors or subordinates have a part to play?

(d) How will you know when it is achieved? (Controls.) What measure, sign or other indication will tell you when you have reached your initial targets?

(e) When was it completed? You fill this in later, with any remarks appropriate. You will get progressively better at planning and directing these sorts of improving activities.

Following this form is a specimen diary which you can use to extract the sections in sequence so that you have a daily/weekly/monthly plan of improvements. Obviously you will need to write out your own form.

The rest is up to you. The book contains a good number of ideas and hints which have helped managers and supervisors to improve themselves and their activities. I can only hope that some of these ideas will prove of value to you, and I do very sincerely wish you every success.

PERSONAL ACTION PLAN (SPECIMEN)

Manager		Date		
Objective	How it is to be achieved	Start date	Controls	Finish date

SPECIMEN DIARY

PROGRAMME FOR:

TASK OR ACTION / WEEK	1 M T W T F	2 M T W T F	3 M T W T F	4 M T W T F	5 M T W T F	6 M T W T F	7 M T W T F	8 M T W T F	NOTES
(LIST TASKS TO BE UNDERTAKEN)	INSERT ✓ FOR ACTION INTENDED OR REQUIRED. CROSS TICK ✗ WHERE ACTION TAKEN. REPLAN OR REMOVE FROM LIST.								

DATE:

PREPARED BY: